SIT-STAND AND KNEEL

CHRIS BELLAND

Unraveling the mysteries of my Catholic faith as a
convert and learning that, God answers in three ways;
Yes, Maybe Later and I have a better plan for you.

DEDICATION

Faith is the realization of what is hoped for and evidence of things not seen. Hebrews 11:1

To My husband Glenn who first felt the call to return to his Catholic roots and led the way to our new life in Christ, opening doors, I never imagined existed.
To My friend in Christ, Barbara who with her strong faith showed me a place to learn about the Catholic Church and hear Him through her words.
To my children, Angelin, Janice, Gabrielle, Gayla, Robert, Lauren, and Vincent who did not judge me, but supported me in my faith journey.
To my parents, Robert and Shirley Hibbard who were committed to their Episcopalian religion and taught their children to be active participants in church at a young age and to live our faith as adults within our church's teachings.

INTRODUCTION

"Can anything good come from Nazareth?" Philip said to
him, "Come and see,"
John 1:46

This book is my story about my Episcopalian upbringing and
ultimate conversion to Catholicism. What happened when
new truths were revealed to me by the Holy Spirit in ways
that I did not know were possible. As I learned about my
Christian faith many questions were answered yet many
more presented themselves.

Along this journey, I have been questioned and chal-
lenged about why I converted and why Catholics do certain
things. These inquiries have made me seek answers and
compare those differences to what I once believed.

As a convert, my lack of knowledge about the Catholic
traditions lead me to question and seek answers that may
seem simple to "cradle Catholics". I have experienced
different parish functions and church truths that have called
me to ask for further clarification. You may have some of

these same questions; Why do the Knights of Columbus wear the plumes? What is a Knight function? What happens when the blessed host is dropped accidentally? What is the big deal about the Blessed Mary? Why don't priests marry? I don't take everything for granted; I learn the why and the when of things. I have come to learn there is a reason for everything. The answer is often from something Jesus did or said.

The title of this book is one of the frequent questions, "Why do Catholics always, SIT, STAND or KNEEL?" When non-Catholics ask this question to a Catholic, the insinuation is, "Make up your mind and go with one of them." I have to smile at that, we have our reasons.

BE NOT AFRAID

Living worthy of the call I received

Ten years ago, my sweet husband, Glenn prayed for an increase in his piety. What? Is that even something we do? God was listening and answering prayers that day and our lives as we knew it, were going to change. Glenn's prayer sounded vague and harmless when he told me months later. But as we soon learned it was the beginning of a change in our lives, our family relationships and an enrichment that we never anticipated. At least I didn't anticipate it. Answered prayer, what a concept.

Glenn decided to look-up his childhood parish and sought reconciliation, and then it was a Quick-step up the aisle, and he was back to his Catholic roots. I was waiting in the car that day for him to come out of the church. He was in there quite a while and I was interested in all that was transpiring, because it was all Greek to me. When he left me in the car his final words were, "Wait here, it will just take a minute, while I talk to the priest." An hour later, he returned, and he had been reconciled for the last thirty years of his life. There were two marriages, two sets of children and many other decisions and life choices that needed to be brought to light. All in all, it was pretty painless, and two hours is not much time to discuss a 30-year hiatus. Maybe, I should say, painless for me. I am not sure how Glenn felt at the time.

When he returned to the car, he explained to me that he could now return to the Catholic church and take communion and that is what he planned to do. He also said, that we could continue to go to both churches and it would be up to me if I wanted to attend the Catholic church with him. When he told me this, I thought- Well, okay, I will come, but I am not going to become Catholic, and I told him so. He was fine with that. As a couple that does everything together, just having my support and companionship at his Catholic service was all he needed at that time.

Prior to his praying for an increase in piety, we were a strong, well, fairly strong Episcopalians. We went to church every Sunday. Why he needed more than that, bewildered me. At our church, we were considered active parishioners. We did more than most people we knew our age. We even attended the non-Sunday events; Pancake suppers, Valentines Dance, volunteered at the cookie table during Social Hour and went to church on Thanksgiving in the Chapel. Primarily, it gave me another reason to see my mom and dad and sit in our pew together every Sunday, the fourth row back from the front on the left. The same people where in front, behind and across from us. We never thought to change. The only time I noticed any change was when years later, I went back for a visit to the Episcopal church after my conversion to Catholicism. It was on a special occasion for my dad and mom, and I noticed my dad no longer sat in that fourth row. He now sat in the rear left about four rows from the back. It was a very sad moment for me. I knew he was struggling with my conversion. It was a struggle for me to hurt them, and I grieved for that.

I love my parents, and they had always been in my corner. They even picked up our kids for church when we didn't want to go so that the kids wouldn't miss. Another change dad made was to have mom say the dinner prayer. It was like he could no longer pray. Mom would hold his hand, and she would say, grace. It was hard to watch — such a change in the family tradition. I was very disheartened over my parent's grief over their feelings of supposed loss of me as a daughter. I know I was the cause of this sadness, but at the same time, I had a new, living zeal for the Lord. A new and exciting thirst for everything biblical.

When I felt the call to join the Catholic church, it also changed how I saw the church and the bible. I now looked forward to reading the Bible, which I had never really done before. I wanted to go to church for Jesus, and not because I wanted to talk to my mom or because I liked a particular priest homily. In fact, my present church, St. Joseph in Battle Creek, has probably had a turnover of 10 different priests in the ten years I have been there. I have loved them all and found each one unique and holy in their own way. But, I have never felt like following one of them to their new assignments. I don't get attached to the priest. I still go to church for Jesus.

Changing churches at first can seem like changing job assignments. I was a nurse at the Veterans Hospital for thirty-one years and had many position changes, and the adapting and newness is similar to that excitement of change. When I switched from being an Episcopal to Catholic, it reminded me of changing from a surgical to the medical floor or one hospital to the next. It is not that you don't value where you were or the friends you have made it is all part of a journey. A faith journey, for me it was digging deeper into the truth of the words of Jesus and his intentions when he set up the church. I was also meeting new people, attending new groups and living experience that my folks did not share while they existed in the same space and time.

One other time I had this feeling of complete life change. When I was 12 years old, we moved from Port Huron to Battle Creek, my dad worked for Grand Trunk Railroad and his job transferred. I recall it was much easier for me to adjust than my "old" best friend Kate, in Port Huron. She was left in kind of a vacuum of a friendless state back in Port Huron, whereas I had lots of new friends in Athens, where we attended school. My transition to the new location went much faster and smoother. I am sure this is the void mom and dad felt, attending the same church every Sunday with no one in the pew but them.

When I sit in our Catholic church with "just" Glenn, I don't feel alone. We believe in the Communion of Saints. The Communion of Saints are all the people in your lives that have gone on before you and are now are saints in heaven. They are there celebrating Mass with you every service. For me, that has always meant my Grandpa Hagan, my moms, dad. He was a fun grandpa. The kind that played baseball with you when he was seventy. He was a devout Catholic and Knight of Columbus. So, when I am at Mass, I am with my grandpa and all others that have died. It is a closeness with the deceased that I have not felt elsewhere.

The other loss for me due to my conversion was the change in the relationship with mom and dad. Our conversations were now guarded when we should have been having exciting discussions about the new changes, new experiences, and joys of my new faith and church life. I was filled with happiness and the Holy Spirit. But, mom and dad couldn't bear to hear it. That hurt them, and so they could not listen, and I could not share. We lost a lot in our relationship with this lack of honesty. The trust that disappears when someone lets you down crumbles the strength of the relationship. It has taken years to regain the love and approval and willingness to be open with what we are doing in our lives. I could not share my new love of God with my folks. In retrospect, wouldn't hearing that your child is happy in the Lord to be something you would cherish? They seemed to shut down, so eventually I didn't ever talk about my faith. No longer sharing my day, or my dreams with them in their kitchen over a cup of tea. That close relationship that we once had, was absent for a long time. I missed that mom was such a great listener and dad loved to give advice. But, it was too hard to see her cry. They couldn't see the difference in our churches, and I couldn't explain it. They took my conversion personally, and it has altered our relationship to this day in many ways. I remember my dad telling me that when he married mom in the Catholic church it altered his relationship with his own father for the rest of his life, a dejavu moment that I wish was not repeated.

I tell you this background, so it will be easier to understand my ambivalence towards joining the Catholic church. Ambivalence is too mild a word; it was downright fear. I had always been the "good daughter." I did well in school, became a nurse because my mom was a nurse, got engaged, but didn't move away from home until I was married. This pattern of pleasing my parents has never left me, and for the most part, it has served me well. My folks are great people, but, to leave the church of my youth, even though I was fifty-two at the time, it was so frightening, I knew it would have to be something divine to make me take that leap. So, for the next three years, we attended the Catholic church then raced over to the Episcopal church, every Sunday. We tried to imply that we were only going to the Episcopal church and just happened to arrive in the nick of time for the Processional each week. In reality, we had been at Mass across the street and had to race over after Communion. Thank God, Catholic Mass is pretty predictable and ends in one hour or less, usually.

My younger brother, Anson, had converted to Catholicism three years earlier, and mom still whispered disdainfully that she thought he had lost his mind. Dad thought he was making the mistake of his life, due to the "controlling nature" of the Catholic church. So, I was not about to tell them about my attending the Catholic church with my husband. Wasn't I just a bystander anyway. I did not feel any compulsion to become Catholic, in those early days. But, subtly I was being made aware of the differences even though it might be similar. What I saw was a deeper sincerity, and the actions were purposeful and had a reason. Prior to this, I never thought anything of the Catholics, good or bad. I was Episcopal, and I didn't see any need to look at other churches. Didn't we all have sacraments? Wasn't the Episcopal church, Catholic Lite? My dad would never agree that we were "Lite" anything, but that Episcopalians were equal if not better. At this time, I was not even praying much about the path I should take. Prayer and including Jesus in my daily life was pretty foreign to me. I didn't include Jesus in my day to day decisions. Afterall, wasn't I college educated and could weigh the pros and cons. I could recognize that there were just too many cons to switch churches. I had not yet heard that it would not be my decision, but the Holy Spirit would call me. The Holy Spirit would "Call me?". As an Episcopalian, we didn't talk much about the Holy Spirit, or I missed that sermon if they did. Now, that I understand that concept, it is much easier to accept my conversion and to empathize with my parents.

The other con was always the idea of thinking about hurting my parents. That was so abhorrent to me. I really didn't want them to know I was sitting in the Catholic church before the Episcopal service. The fear of them finding out was always on my mind. I imagined feeling like Judas after he had taken the silver.

One Saturday afternoon I was at mom and dad's visiting, and Glenn called, "Did you forget we are going to Mass at 5:00 pm?" Oh, yes, I did! I made some lame excuse to mom and dad that I had to leave abruptly and raced out. Let the lying begin. Not sure if I was sheltering them or protecting myself.

But then it happened...

I had a dream. A vision I prefer to call it, and it was clear, vivid and detailed. I was at St. Joseph Catholic Church, like everyone else, I was kneeling in the pews, praying. I looked up, and John Paul II was coming in, lying on a gurney, entering on Mary's side in the front of the church. St. John Paul II was laying on a satin, cushiony sheet which draped to the floor, it seemed to be floating on its own accord. At first, I thought he was dead or asleep; his eyes were closed. Then Pope John Paul slowly sat up, looked out over the congregation and made eye contact with me. Everyone else was still praying and did not notice him. He extended his right hand to me, palm up. He opened his fingers and beckoned me with them. He then said, " Do not be afraid, come." He smiled. I looked at him, and I was shocked. Then I turned my head to see what others around me thought, but everyone was still head bowed and praying. I was the only one that was seeing him. The only one with which he made eye contact. The only one with whom he was to speak. I started to cry. The vision was over, and I knew what it meant.

It was at that moment that I knew I was called to join the Catholic church. I was no longer on the fence about it. I was no longer afraid. I was sure. I knew I must put my love of God before family.

I have come to set the earth on fire, and how I wish It was already blazing!... From now on a household of five will be divided, three against two and two against three, a father will be divided against his son and a son against his father, a mother against her daughter and a daughter against her mother, a mother-in-law against her daughter-

in-law and a daughter-in-law against her mother-in-law.
Luke 12:49, 52-53

I drove to my parents' home. I felt so determined and strong in my decision. I did not want to delay sharing my news or starting my new journey to become a Catholic. On the way to their house, I turned on the radio and what music should be playing? You know it, "Be not afraid"... "I go before you always. Come follow me. I will give you rest". I guess God wanted to be sure I knew it was not a mistake, not a coincidence, but a divine answer. I have put Jesus first since that day and have accepted any changes in relationships, and over time they have smoothed out.

My parents were at their round kitchen table in the kitchen. Happy for my unexpected visit. Then I dropped the bomb. I didn't sit down. I kind of blurted out that I wanted to join the Catholic Church. I won't forget the silence around the kitchen table. The lack of eye contact heads down. Then dad said, " That's up to you, but you are making a mistake, they are very controlling. I never want to hear or speak about it again." After an awkward silence, I left. Dad's words have not proven true for me. I have found my Catholic faith very freeing and supportive. But, I know he spoke from an unresolved pain of long past and hadn't reconciled that yet. Over the years of awkward silence, tears, missed dinners and uncomfortable religious holidays our relationship is healing. I will always have deep love and gratitude towards my parents for starting me on my faith journey. Their strong faith and commitment to attending church and becoming involved in church groups and activities have made me the strong Catholic I am today.

What I have learned since becoming a Catholic is that I didn't choose to become Catholic. I opened my heart to the possibility and Jesus. The Holy Spirit called me home to the Catholic church. This belief that it wasn't me has gone a long way in me not feeling guilty if one of my kids is not Catholic. I can only be a good role model. I can plant seeds, live the Catholic life and aspire to be more holy. Maybe, someone will see something I do. Maybe they will think that they want that feeling or way of life or the better way and look into the Catholic faith. It is the Holy Spirits job to call them home. I try to tell everyone to pray for that open heart and to ask for Gods guidance. Allowing Him to make changes, heal and soften stubborn ideas that are seen as facts. I still pray that my folks' hearts will be softened towards me and accept me as I am and be proud that I am a Catholic. I will always honor my parents, as this is honoring God.

I have talked to others, and not everyone has a "vision" or an experience that they can remember. A moment, if you will, that becomes the turning point for them to want to join the Catholic Church. God must have known I was one of those "stiff-necked" people. A throwback to the Israelites, stubborn and hard to lead. I know this to be true. My dad would point this out when we danced together, and he would say to me, " Christine, you are so difficult to lead." I guess he was used to mom. Once, being stubborn almost cost me my life.

I was in a motorcycle accident because I didn't trust the driver on a curve and so did not lean into the curve with him, as I should have. We were going fast, well at least that is what I thought at the time. Anyway, we had an accident, and

Thanks be to God, we were both alright. The moment when I was going through the air, flying off the bike and I was suspended in time and it seemed like slow motion. The green from the trees was so vivid to my eyes and I had so many thoughts at once in my head which I had time to sort out and I remember thinking, "when you land, fall so that you don't break your neck," so, I did. I landed on my back but felt like I couldn't move. The first thing I did was take my left thumb and moved it to touch my wedding ring. I was so relieved that I was not paralyzed. From that moment on I knew I would be alright. Trust might be an issue with me. Glenn, God bless him can lead me when we dance, that is until we took formal dance lessons. Now, neither of us can dance.

Regarding the vision, God knew me. He blessed me with this undeniable vision. I was convinced once I had the vision and have never looked back or regretted my decision. My advice for most people would, "Don't wait for a vision." God doesn't work by proving himself to us daily. He is not one to prove his existence by deeds, although once you are attuned to Him, you can see Him in everything. A favorite scripture points out this fact when Jesus speaks to doubting Thomas.

Then he said to Thomas, "Put your finger here and see my hands, and bring your hand and put it into my side, and do not be unbelieving, but believe," Jesus said to him, "Have you come to believe because you have seen me? Blessed are those who have not seen and have believed." John 20: 27-29

Ten years have passed, and my folks and I don't discuss

our religious differences, but the love and concern for each other are back. I hope they see me as someone of strong faith. Someone they can say- we helped her become who she is today. She just happens to be Catholic.

I find I am still that young girl that will always want their approval and unconditional love

2

MARY WHO?

Experiencing the presence of our Blessed Mother nearby

As an Episcopalian, I didn't think much about our Blessed Mother. I knew Jesus mothers name was Mary, but that is about all. I didn't pray to the Blessed Mother as an intercessor for my prayers, I didn't understand I was one of her children, and I didn't know she loved me as Jesus does. I didn't think anything bad of her; she was more like a nameless substitute teacher that didn't have anything to offer me when my favorite teacher was not there.

Since becoming Catholic I have had a couple of very memorable first-hand experiences with Our Blessed Mother, and they have helped me to develop my relationship with Her and I want to share this closeness we can all have with those I know.

Most of my family are non-Catholic, and I am sure they would feel like I used to. It would be like not knowing you would like something because you never tried it. For instance, take elotes, or Mexican corn. At our house we had regular sweet corn with butter and salt, but once I tried an elote. I was at the Superfest, a carnival at St. Joseph Parish and there were many ethnics cuisines there. At the Mexican table, elotes were sold. They are an ear of sweet corn, cooked, then covered with Mayonnaise and Tajin powder and Parmesan Cheese. Does that sound spicy, or good or would you stay away from it? Well, I love to try new food, so I bought one, and I found it so delicious, I bought another. I also, purchased the spices at a store so if I want I can make them at home. If someone had told me to eat corn with mayonnaise, I might have passed it by. It pays to try new things, and that is like introducing the Blessed Mary to people. You may think you don't want or need her, but it is because you have never tried Her.

One time when at St. Joseph's church, kneeling, head down and eyes closed I was made aware of the overpowering, beautiful scent of flowers. Now, this was in the middle of a service, and no new people had come to sit in the pews near me or walked by. That was my first thought. It was someone passing by with a strong, sweet perfume and I just noticed it. But no, everyone was praying quietly. I asked Glenn if he smelled it, he said, "No." Which I found hard to believe, it was such a lovely smell. The smell was so sweet, so memorable, I have since read that it was probably roses. Our Lady is known for Her association with the scent of roses when she is near. It was peaceful and the most pleasant smell. I have not smelled that exact smell again, but I am waiting for her to come close, so I can.

The next occasion of my close exposure to the real presence of our Blessed Mother was when we were visiting our son, Rob in Hawaii. He took us to a huge Catholic church, with the parking lot beneath the church structure. I guess, real-estate is so expensive they build this way. We arrived early, and I noticed that there was a line of people, especially couples waiting to walk up to the statue of the Blessed Virgin Mary. My hubby and I got in the line. As we drew closer I realized that the couples were standing under the statue and touching her feet, while they prayed. When we got up to her, we did the same. She was a life-size figure in sandals. Her sandals were at eye level. We both reached out, eyes closed and touched her toes. When I brushed her skin with my fingertips, I immediately, opened my eyes and looked up to her face to see if she had come alive. The porcelain on her toes felt like skin. Real skin. It felt warm, soft and supple. I was convinced I was in the presence of the Blessed Mother. This moment with the Blessed Mary confirms I need to follow Jesus.

His mother said to the servants, "Do whatever he tells you." John 2:5

When we sat down, I asked Glenn, if he felt her skin too? He seemed confused by the question. I told him, her skin felt real. I then repeated my question. "Didn't you feel it? Her feet being real?" He is a smart man, and he calmly said, "We all see and feel different things when we need to. I believe you felt that". He hadn't felt that quality to her toes but did not doubt that I had. That answer in itself was a revelation to me. I always thought everyone experienced faith, in the same way, believed the same way. It makes more sense that God speaks to us as we need to hear him, in ways and methods that we can relate. Mary becomes very real to me in Hawaii.

Since that time, I have attended seminars on Mary and been consecrated to Mary through the Legion of Mary in our parish and have built a relationship with her. When I pray for my children, it is through Mary. We often say, "To Jesus through Mary." My children are Mary's children. She loves them more than me and knows their joys and pains. She understands and knows what they need and what hardships they are going through. She loves me and only wants my happiness.

Many Churches have a separate or smaller chapel area called the adoration chapel which is for adoring Jesus. In Adoration chapels, there will be a life-size statue of the Blessed Virgin Mary on the left flank of the altar. She is usually up on a pedestal so that her feet are at your eye level. She is often wearing a blue robe holding a Rosary and crushing Satan depicted by a snake under her feet. What I like to do is walk up to her so that I can look right up into her face. She is looking down, and her gaze is steady. She looks like she is looking at me. Her eyes are compassionate, all knowing, loving and she has a listening demeanor. I love to stand there and connect with Mother Mary. I try to do this when no one else is in the chapel; it may seem strange to others. Secondly, we are not supposed to walk up in the altar area. So, I do it discreetly, when I am alone with her, she is so lovely. You all should try it sometime. It is a tender experience that will help you gain a love for the Blessed Mary.

Just in case there is any confusion that I idolize Our Lady, that would not be true. I revere her. I imagine what she has seen, felt. To know you are carrying the Son of God, raising the Son of God and know you will see your son die and be helpless to stop it. What strength she had. She was only a young woman at the time. Secondly, we don't idolize statue's or saints or anything else in the Catholic church. We ask them to carry our prayers to Jesus or to pray for us. If you are thinking about how this can be done, think of it this way. Has a friend ever asked you to pray for them? "Pray for me; I am having a rough week." Your friend trusts that you will pray for them and it will help them. They are certainly not idolizing you or giving you any super human prayer powers. They believe in the power of prayer.

When I became a mother, raising sons, you realize there is a special love, that is different than the love you have for your daughters. Maybe you realize very early that one day, you won't be the most important person to them, so you need to develop that loving relationship when they are young. I always felt that my girls would make every effort to come home for a visit or call. Sons will be cleaved to their wives, but they will retain that early closeness in their hearts to their mothers and feel sweet love and need for approval from afar. Most sons listen to their mothers, tend to care for their mothers and demonstrate loving compassion, almost protective nature towards their mothers. I know mine do. I also know that my sons listen to me and if I should ask them to do something for me, they will try there hardest to complete it. When I think of that mother-son relationship, it is no wonder I want to pray through Mary to Jesus. It is like speed dialing, and He will pay special attention to that phone call. After all, it's His mom.

3

THE ROSARY MYSTERY

Learning to see Jesus through his Mothers eyes

I had not heard of a Rosary before becoming Catholic. I think mom had one but didn't share it. I asked her for some beads once, and I kind of ran across it but didn't want to break it up for its parts. Some of the ladies at the Episcopal church were using prayer beads to pray, and I needed to string some together for myself to use. Since, that time I have of course learned that prayer beads are more self-directed, more intercessional. When praying for yourself, I am not sure when or if one included praying prayers for Jesus or any traditional prayers. I never did learn of any method or instructions to praying with prayer beads. I literally abandoned that form of praying, because it did not provide the routine I required to become my "go-to" prayer that I needed during a time of struggle or when I hurriedly needed a prayer, not something where I had to think of who or what I needed to pray for and why.

I became aware of the Catholic church when I was

working as a Home Care Nurse at the Battle Creek Veterans Hospital, through a nurse I met there, Barbara. When we would both be at the office and not on calls, we would take walks outdoors for our breaks. Barbara was a strong Catholic, and I was a firm Episcopalian at that time. We would talk a lot about the Lord and our different views and differences in faith on these walks. One day she asked if I wanted to learn the Hail Mary. I hadn't ever heard it, so I said yes. The prayer appealed to me from the get-go, and she taught me line by line. I am not a very good memorizer and learning simple prayers take me what seems forever. But, I finally learned it and could say it without stumbling. The simplicity of this prayer appealed to me and found this prayer helpful in stressful situations. I would say it over and over in my head while in the dentist chair. It was easy, short and I could repeat it without struggling to remember it. Sitting in the dentist chair this prayer, distracted me and took my mind to another place while the drilling for a filling was going on. Over time I learned, I could talk to Mary, and that she was real and not just a person in a picture on the wall or in a book.

Barbara invited Glenn and I to several church seminars, and we attended a two-year Discipleship to learn about the life and times of Jesus and his lineage back to Adam. I was probably the only non-Catholic in the class, but that was okay. I was welcomed and learned so much but didn't feel the actual call to become a Catholic and leave the Episcopal church. Believe me; I wanted to feel the call of the Holy Spirit. I was tired of attending both churches or at least the mad rush and conspiracy involved in attending two different churches. But I did not have that strong urge to change my life, nor did Glenn push me to make a change. He would ask me on occasion, "Do you feel like you could join the Catholic church yet?" but my answer was always, "Nope, I'll let you know. Sorry." The fear was still greater than the reward, or so I thought. Now, I realize that I am here on earth to do Gods work and to do what it takes to obtain entry into the promised eternal life. The insight of eternal life is the end all and is a new thing for me. I mean, I knew I believed in heaven, and I wanted to end up there. But the concept that everything I do on earth must either prepare me for eternal life or smooth my path towards Eternal Life is new. This new recognition of the importance of eternal life and working towards it helps me to understand the lack of socialization that visitors may see at Catholic churches. Catholics attend Mass and go home. There is not a lot of social chit chat. Like my granddaughter, Joysa says, "Let's go to the quiet church." Well, it is quiet, because people are praying in the church. We are not there to talk about the weather or our families, while others may be praying. No one wants to disturb others. The secular conversation is encouraged outside of the church. That doesn't mean that I don't know the people in my church. When I look around, I can name or give some detail about most people in the pews. I didn't learn this from the coffee hour, however, because, that is a no-show most times. One would think yummy donuts or even the Knights of Columbus breakfast after Masses, would be standing room only, but not so much.

When you want to get to know the people that sit in the pews of the church, you must join activities, groups and become integral to the smooth running of the Mass. Each Mass and we have five a weekend and then of course daily

Mass, can have 4-6 Ushers, 4-12 acolytes, two lay readers, 3-7 Eucharistic Ministers, 1-2 Priest or Deacons, one cantor and at specific Masses there will be choirs. That is 90 to 100 people volunteering to serve every weekend. On special occasions, it is not unusual to see four priests, two deacons, 12-15 acolytes, and then the women's groups put on the meals or snacks and that is attended by parishioners that you get to know. Outside of the general running of the Mass, there will always be seminars, or additional services, adoration and then there are the women's and men's groups, rosary groups or Reconciliation. At these activities is when you really get to know the congregation. As you can see to the visitor it may look like we are not social or don't care for each other but in reality, we love our parish and we all play a role in its success and stability and we are all called to do more.

> Should anyone press you into service for one mile, go with him for two miles. Give to the one who asks of you, and do not turn your back on one who wants to borrow. Matthew 8:41-42

Once Glenn reverted to his Catholic faith our free time involved church activities. In the three-year period before I joined the church and since then we have spent our vacation times visiting Monasteries, or Marian Centers, Catholic conferences and other Holy sites. In my heart, I had become a believer in Catholicism, and of course, Glenn was a fervent revert to the Church. Our life was rich, our conversations never dull, and our house had a transformation which our daughter Lauren once remarked as, "It's like a shrine in here,

I can't even bring friends over!' We laughed at the time but, it was true. We had different items around the house to remind us of different things of our faith. We also went to a lot of souvenir shops in our travels and picked up our share of items.

One of my treasured souvenirs was a Rosary which had the name of each mystery on the Our Father beads. This labeled rosary helped me, so I didn't have to look them up as I was reciting the rosary. I just read the mystery for the day. That is still one of my most cherished rosaries. I obtained that in Hanceville, Georgia when we visited the Eternal Word Television Network (EWTN) site. Mother Angelica was a nun of the Poor Clare's of Perpetual Adoration, and she founded the Our Lady of Angels Monastery in Irondale, Alabama. The monastery is very sprawling, in a rural setting. The driveway up to the monastery is a mile long or so, with white fence and fields with animals grazing, so beautiful. There is also one of the biggest souvenir shops you probably will ever see. The building looks like a castle. In this souvenir shop is where I purchased the unique rosary with the mysteries labeled on the Our Father bead. This monastery is a place to visit, even though it is off the beaten track a little.

When people go to Mass, the ladies often wear coverings on their heads, mantillas. Mantillas are interesting in them-selves. Traditionally, they are of lace, and they may have religious figures in the lace. For unmarried women, white is usually the color of lace worn, and for married women, they wear black lace. But, I have seen them in all colors. When I was a young girl, and we attended St. Paul's Episcopal Church in Port Huron, mom would always cover my sister

Anita's head and mine with a doily or hanky or something for the church service. This custom of reverence seems to be coming back in Catholic churches at this time and if you ever go to a High Latin Mass, wearing the veil can be commonplace. Also, women wear dresses, no shorts. If you visit the Vatican in Rome, they sell scarves outside in the courtyard so that the visitors can tie the scarf around their hips to cover their legs, in case they are wearing shorts or short skirts or maybe have bare shoulders. They won't even let you into St. Peters Basilica without the proper attire of respect.

Now that I had an actual Rosary, one would think I might use it every day. I did find saying the traditional rosary a little long, and I had to reference what I was saying or meditating on frequently. It didn't come easy. I was also still working every day, and I hadn't built in any consistent prayer times in those early days. Becoming good at anything takes practice, and some exploration on what works for you, your schedule and your family commitments is a must. It is easy to get discouraged and think it is too hard to give God the praise and worship He deserves. Luckily, I had Barbara, as an experienced Catholic and close friend and she showed me another way. Was it luck? Or was it God speaking through her. I tend to believe the later. As Glenn often says, "God speaks through other people to us, if we are willing to listen."

I adapted my daily schedule to include time for consistent prayer. Before work I would get up about 4:30 to be able to complete my prayers and say a Rosary, before breakfast and getting ready to head to work. The rosary usually takes 17-20 minutes to pray. Honestly, I found that I did not have that much uninterrupted time in the morning. So, my friend Barbara who seems to know all things Catholic shared with me the prayers of the Divine Mercy Chaplet. This chaplet is a devotion to Jesus Christ associated with the apparitions of Jesus to Saint Faustina Kowalska, a Polish nun and mystic. The focus of this chaplet is the merciful love of God and the desire to let that love and mercy come from the one praying it to those that need it. We even celebrate Divine Mercy Sunday, the Sunday after Easter and pray this devotion at church. It is the easiest Devotion to start with because there is very little to memorize and only takes about seven minutes to complete. I love it, and it has become another one of my go-to prayers.

This Divine Mercy Chaplet devotion is a repetition of two different prayers.

On the larger Our Father beads, one prays-

Eternal Father, I offer you the body and blood, soul and divinity of your dearly beloved son, our Lord Jesus Christ in atonement for our sins and those of the whole world.

On the Hail Mary Beads, one prays-

For the sake of His sorrowful Passion have mercy on us and on the whole world

Like the traditional Rosary, you use Rosary beads. But the prayers are shorter. The seven minutes fit much better into my morning schedule. I was still using my Rosary beads just different prayers attached to them. The Divine Mercy Chaplet is an official prayer, so it wasn't like I was cheating; it was not the traditional Rosary.

Traditional Rosary is a method of helping us remember important events in the history of our salvation. These events are called "Mysteries." There are 20 different mysteries that we reflect on when we pray the rosary. These mysteries are divided into four different categories; Joyful, Luminous, Sorrowful and Glorious. Of course, there are many other important events in the life of Our Lord, but these twenty speak to his life with his Mother. The Rosary is said to be viewing Jesus's life through the eyes of his Mother.

The Rosary beads consist of a crucifix, then three beads, then a larger Our Father bead followed by the ten Hail Mary beads, which is often called a decade. This sequence of praying on the beads is repeated five times then you get back to the "tail" with the three single beads and the crucifix. The five Our Father beads are set apart or a little larger than the twenty Hail Mary beads. One is praying the Our Father five times and the Hail Mary fifty times on the circle of the Rosary.

Large bead- Pray the Lord's Prayer.

Our Father which art in Heaven, hallowed be thy Name. Thy Kingdom come. Thy will be done. On earth, as it is in heaven. Give us this day our daily bread. And forgive us our trespasses, as we forgive those that trespass against us. And lead us not into temptation but deliver us from evil. For thine is the Kingdom, the Power, and the Glory, forever and ever. Amen.

Smaller decade beads-Pray a Hail Mary

Hail Mary full of Grace, the Lord is with thee. Blessed are thou among women and blessed is the fruit of the womb Jesus. Holy Mary Mother of God pray for us sinners now and at the hour of our death. Amen.

The Rosary is a means of meditation as well as prayer and the mysteries of the rosary are based on scripture. The trick is to say it while praying or reflecting on the mystery of the decade. It takes practice to do this. It is like doing two things at once, well maybe three things, because, you are moving the rosary beads with each prayer, saying the Hail Mary, and reflecting on the mystery. I find when I do this in public, my mind will go blank and I can't recall the words to the Hail Mary, which is a prayer I know as well as my name. It can be embarrassing, but everyone helps to remind you of the words. We do the rosary in public at Mass or funerals. I admire those people that can lead the rosary in public, what courage. I would stumble, and I know the words. Stage fright is a very real thing. Thanks be to God for those that can pray the Rosary publicly, or really, to pray spontaneously at all. As a former Episcopalian or a Catholic, this has never been an easy thing to do. I admire those folks that are good public prayerers, if that's a word. At my son Rob's wedding, his mother-in-law, a Mormon, did the before meal prayer. It was so inclusive, complete and personal just outstanding. There is something to be said for this form of prayer. As a Catholic I do love rote prayer though. Everyone can say it, everyone knows it, there is nothing unexpected and even children can participate. Our granddaughter, Joysa, will let no one else say grace when she is over, of course, it is the Catholic prayer, and she does it all with the beginning and ending Father, Son, and Holy Ghost.

The mysteries of the rosaries can be quite a mystery, but they are quite simple. An example of one of the Joyful mysteries is "The Visitation," Elizabeth was filled with the Holy Spirit and cried out in a loud voice; "Blest are you among women and blessed is the fruit of your womb." I would try to keep that thought in mind while I recited the Hail Mary. I thought I was a good multi-tasker. But, truthfully, I have decided we can only do one thing well. An example of my multi-tasking inadequacy is, when I am driving the car, I find it difficult to carry on the conversation without steering off the road or forgetting where I am even going. Or, when cooking, I may be watching the eggs, but burning the toast. My inability to multitask is why I have Glenn help to set the table or pour the milk. It all becomes too much at times. Maybe, I am just getting old. That's a scary thought. Not the getting old part but being inadequate or inefficient. Being dependent on others is always an iffy situation.

Lately, we have been praying the Scriptural Rosary. A scriptural rosary is the same Rosary, but between each Hail Mary, we also read a piece of scripture that corresponds to the mystery, beautiful. It doesn't take much longer and is a much richer rosary.

There you have it. Hopefully, the mystery is made simpler. The Rosary is a beautiful and meditative tool to use in prayer life. I like to pray it during Adoration when I am alone with Jesus or before the beginning of Mass or at Funerals. The recommendation is that we pray the rosary daily. I will admit, I like that idea, but have yet to put it into practice. Recently, I found a new phone app. called Broken Mary. This is an audio Rosary prayed by Kevin Matthews a writer and radio personality who attributes life changes to his relationship with a Broken Mary statue and his struggles in life. This app is simple to listen to in the car. I tend to hear and pray the rosary more frequently now.

I may have started with that one Rosary, but in the last ten years, we have learned to make them. Glenn is especially good at it and has made me ten or so. He makes them from metal or rope, often giving them away. He has made each of the kids a house rosary where the Hail Mary beads are one-inch wooden balls. Do they all have them hanging on their walls? No, but that is their call, house rosaries may be an acquired taste. I find that young people have color schemes to their homes and asymmetry to their wall furnishings. That is not something I never did. I have whatever I like in my home, and I make any additions match.

Another interesting rosary is our yard rosary which Glenn made from wooden balls that are two inches in diameter. I told you we loved the rosary. This is the rosary that is draped between our Mary statue on our front walk and down the flower bed.

Our latest acquisitions were from Fatima Portugal. We went there last year and picked up some treasures from the Fatima Shrine. We were on a cruise ship and had a Port of Call in Lisbon. When we looked at the daily excursions, we realized there was a day-long excursion out to Fatima, Portugal to the Shrine of Fatima. We couldn't believe our luck. Okay, it was a divine interruption of our cruise, now we know that. The Shrine of Fatima is sprawling and reminded me of St. Peters Cathedral in the Vatican City, very peaceful. There was some beautiful choir music playing across the square and organ notes lingering on the air. Another lady on tour turned to me and said, " Do you feel the peace here?" I knew what she meant; the peacefulness was palpable and brought tears to my eyes. I could not believe I was there; we hadn't planned on it.

We did attend Mass there; the church was full and so diverse, it was in Portuguese, but it didn't matter, we understood the service, Mass is Mass. We could follow along in

29

English, and we knew our responses. The shrine area was strictly for praying. There were no vending areas, which was in itself very respectful. All souvenir shops were outside the shrine. We spent the day at the memorial, often just sitting outside in the square, in the sun and light breeze, enjoying the milieu. Very special, and unforgettable.

My son Robert brought me back a beautiful rosary from the Vatican before I could go there. He was in the military and had a couple of days leave and went to Rome. Now, he is not Catholic. I thought it especially thoughtful that he purchased a Vatican rosary for me because at that time I had no idea I would ever be able to go there.

I now have many rosaries in different colors. I can coordinate the colors of them with my clothing if I choose, I have so many, and I love them. I don't think there is a personal limit. We always have one handy to give to someone in need or at a new grandchild's birth. I admire those people that can lead the rosary in public.

4

SITTING WITH JESUS

Listening for God's whisper

People will ask me if I hear God, well, not exactly. But, I get ideas or thoughts that I know I need to act on and I know they are from God. These thoughts can be comforting and make me feel good or nagging and require action. It is like a conscience, but the words are not usually directed at something for me but what I should be doing for others. An outward action is needed to complete and make whole the thought.

Glenn and I sit with our Lord in the Seton Chapel at St. Phil once a week, as adorers. This practice of Perpetual Adoration was a new thing to me as a Catholic. My friend Barbara introduced me to it before I became a Catholic. I would go an hour before work and sit in the chapel for a silent time of prayer and center myself. This practice helped me get through a lot of work struggles and also sort out my work week or plan what I needed to accomplish for the weekend. It is quite a luxury to have an hour to yourself, at any time. I recall when Glenn and I were first married, and we would have all five kids together, it could be very over-whelming and loud. There would be times I would lock myself in the bathroom, draw a bath and have a cup of tea and relax in the quiet. It was the only way to be alone without the traffic of little feet and their questions. What I remember is that it seemed Glenn would rap on the door and ask quietly if, "Are you alright?" in a very nervous voice. I am not sure if he was anxious because he was alone out there with all of the kids or he was afraid I would never come out of the bathroom sane again. I can smile now, but it wasn't easy blending two young families. For those that have done it, you know the challenges but ultimately the joys that come along with this new marital arrangement.

Many Catholic parishes will have a Chapel, and some will have it designated as an Adoration Chapel when they have the Blessed Sacrament exposed. To a non-Catholic that is a wild thought in itself. It all reverts to Catholics believing in the conversion or transubstantiation of the Body and Blood of Christ where the bread and wine become the Body and Blood of Christ. Actually, turn in to Jesus himself. As we sit in the chapel, we adore what to a non-Catholic would appear to be a wafer of bread in a pseudo gold holder and be reverent while doing it. But, that in essence is Adoration of the Blessed Sacrament. The Catholic faith is all about the mystery of the Transformation of bread and wine into the body and blood of Christ. We take this fact so seriously that we guard our Lord after the Transformation. The blessed hosts are placed in a locked Tabernacle on the altar. Only the priests or Eucharistic Ministers have the approval to unlock and remove Blessed Sacraments. We don't distribute our

Lord as the Blessed Sacrament to non-Catholics. One must be in full Communion with the Church and its teachings.

If a blessed host is accidentally dropped during Mass, there is a special procedure to pick up the blessed sacrament and dispose of it. There is a designated sink in the Sanctuary that does not drain into the public sewer system but straight into the ground. It is for washing your hands after you have touched the Blessed hosts. We return any part of Jesus to the ground, not an unknown receptacle. Eucharistic Ministers or the lay people that distribute the body and blood of Jesus during the Eucharist are specially trained. Glenn and I are Eucharistic Ministers and assist the Priest at Mass once or twice a month. We have been trained to refer questionable communicants to the priest. One has to be of sound mind, a Catholic, of the age of reason, which is seven years old and had their first Communion.

One time, there was a woman with dementia that came up for Communion, but she was doing repetitive actions with her hands, and couldn't make the appropriate responses so instead of receiving the blessed host, she was given a blessing instead. She did not receive the blessed host during Mass, because we weren't sure she was going to consume it. She might have dropped it or given it away. This is not to say that when the blessed sacrament is taken into homes it is not given. Homes are a more controlled environment. When we were at the Nursing home giving Communion to the aged and some dementia patients we had a procedure if they didn't complete the act of consumption, if they became confused and didn't want to consume the Blessed Host., we would consume it or bury it. It was never left to chance. The Blessed Host is Jesus we are talking about. That is always how you must think about Blessed sacraments. We don't carry Him around in our pocket or go thru drive-thru's or hold onto Him for hours. We take the Blessed Sacrament in a designated container, called pix and protect it on our person and drive straight to the site where we are to distribute the sacrament.

In the Adoration Chapel the priest has blessed and already transformed the host into the Body of Christ and placed it in the Monstrance, the golden holder. It will sit atop the altar with someone in attendance until the Priest returns and removes it and places it back into the locked Tabernacle. The tabernacle is the sacred little house for Jesus, usually on the back altar. It contains blessed and non-blessed hosts until they are needed.

Adoration Chapel is often one of the best places to hear the voice of God. When we are in adoration, we are the only ones there with Jesus for that hour. There will be people that come in to pray and then leave, but it is our honor to sit with Jesus for that hour. When Jesus is exposed(out of the tabernacle), he is never to be left alone. As I sit there and open my heart to his word, my mind does ramble, but I call it back and repeat this phrase, "Jesus your servant is listening." Then I listen.

Then the Lord said, "Go outside and stand on the mountain before the Lord; the Lord will be passing by," A strong and heavy wind was rending the mountains and crushing rocks before the mountains and crushing rocks before the Lord- but the Lord was not in the wind. After the wind there was an earthquake- but the Lord was not in the earthquake. After the earthquake there was fire- but the Lord was not in the fire. After the fire there was a tiny whispering sound. When he heard this, Elijah hid his face his cloak and went and stood at the entrance of the cave. A voice said to him, "Elijah, why are you here?". 1King 19:11-13

I may pray the Rosary or read a religious book. I have even brought my granddaughter, Joysa and we pray or read. It is a peaceful, precious hour. There is a book in the chapel with anonymous intentions written. People will write in their concerns, fears, pleadings, gratitude's and ask others to pray for their issues. It is always a revelation to me when I read it. It proves you cannot judge a book by its cover. One never knows the pain inside others or their fears. Someone has money problems, or their daughter has a brain tumor, or their Dad has died. So many different spiritual needs for prayer. Reading the intentions in this book tends to soften my heart towards all humanity. These words could be by anyone's; it could be the person sitting in front of me at Mass or the Usher smiling and helping others to their seats. It could be the Priest. Unlike Facebook where everything is public; our inner anxieties and hurts are often only for God to see. Secondly, it confirms how very blessed my life is. My gratitude so outweighs my pains.

Thoughts or ideas that come to me while in Adoration are often actions I need to follow up on to check on people I know. These actions include offering comfort or support, to make others feel they are not alone but remembered. For example; Call your cousin, see how they are. Pray for your niece. Send a "Miss you" card to your friend with a prayer card inserted. Forgive and clear the air with your daughter. These are thoughts, only fleeting thoughts. They come quickly and can be as easily forgotten unless followed up with action. That is the key. When you hear the soft whisper of Gods voice, he usually wants you to carry out something. Carrying out the action and extending God's love to another is the second Commandment. The first is to Love Him and the second is to love each other. God is all love, and we are here to be the eyes, ears, hands, and actions of His love many times.

Yes, He speaks to us outside the walls of a church. God is everywhere. We as the people are God's church. But, talking to God is not enough. We rely too much on our own direction and opinion of right and wrong. In essence, we become our own God. We are writing our own truths and rules for living. Relying on only our own thoughts and guidance is why we all need the community of our parish and the guidance of our priests and the role models of active laity. The church's teaching, reading of scripture, breaking of the bread and religious teaching all help us to live out Gods plan, not our own.

Another truth is the question of, "What sacraments are we getting outside of the Church walls?" Maybe, you aren't aware of sacraments, what they are, why they are important, why God instituted them, how sacraments benefit us and make a living in a secular world doable while living Gods laws. There are seven sacraments in the Catholic Church, these are, Baptism, Confirmation, Eucharist, Penance, Anointing of the Sick, Marriage and Holy Orders. Sacraments give us the grace of God to us. We might find the peace of God sitting by a lake or admiring works of religious art or cuddling a puppy, but we can never revere animals or nature over God. Only God can give us His love, His grace that helps us through our day. He makes us feel loved and complete and worthy of love by others. We all need His grace, as often as we can.

> So, let us confidently approach the throne of grace to receive mercy and to find grace for the timely help. Hebrews 4: 10

Let me mention how important the sacrament of Baptism is because recently I have heard someone say, they weren't sure it was necessary. This person, "Felt right with God, without it." Well, God created baptism for a reason. After the fall of Adam and Eve, we all had that "original sin," on us. The sin of our forefathers was forever passed down to all the innocent offspring. That would be us. Baptism forgives all sins, original and personal sins as well as all punishment for sin at the time of baptism. Baptism is essential for salvation and is a foundation for all Christians to be in communion with each other. We are reborn as children of God in baptism. Jesus himself insisted on being baptized, as were all of his disciples and followers. Baptism places an indelible mark, a mark that never comes off, on our soul and this sign on our soul, that marks us as Christ's own forever.

I pray that for those that are not baptized or don't understand the need for baptism. I pray that they reconsider and not take the sacrament of baptism lightly. Also, parents, do not baptize your children by yourselves in their baths, or while swimming without an ordained minister. Do not risk the salvation of your loved ones, encourage them to be baptized legitimately. Love your children enough to do what God demonstrated to us and desires for us.

Regarding hearing Gods voice, it is true, we all hear Gods promptings everywhere, every day. Maybe these voices we hear are often our conscience. My conscience is usually the voice of reason, "Don't eat that; you don't need a value meal, get up and exercise or even... pray or pick up the house," You get it, all the things that I probably don't relish and don't act on. But, when I hear thoughts about other people I tend to take more notice and want to follow through. I often write down what I am supposed to do, to help remember it. That is how this book came to print. I had heard the whisper of God tell me to share my story many times in the past but did not have the courage or knowledge on how to make it happen. What direction should I take? Then, He gave me the idea to write my dad's memoirs. Writing dad's memoirs had a least five benefits; 1) Dad could share his life story with posterity so his life history would not be lost 2) the interviews and recording of the memoirs would give me a reason to see my dad and mom weekly, reconnecting, laughing and sometimes crying over dad's memories, 3) the time with dad may remind my dad that I am the same person even though I am not an Episcopalian anymore 4) it would demonstrate my never-ending love for my dad and mom and 5) I learned how to publish a book using my author daughter, Ellie Wade's contacts. Praise God for her ground-breaking book writing skills.

I am writing this book about my conversion story, learning the marvels of the Catholic faith and the significance of what I do and say on my salvation. As I have learned, one should not ignore God's signs or whispers.

5

TEARS OF THE HOLY SPIRIT

An unexpected and uncontrollable meltdown.

One day we decided to attend Mass at the Capuchins monastery in Detroit. It was here that I experienced the Weeping of the Holy Spirit which I found unexpected and embarrassing. In my early years as a Catholic we traveled to many sacred sites, one of which was the Capuchin Monastery in Detroit, Michigan. This monastery is the home and burial site of Blessed Solanus Casey, who was beatified, and made a Saint by the Catholic church in 2017. Blessed Solanus was a servant of the people, a porter of this monastery, he encouraged everyone to, "Thank God ahead of time." He had died in 1957 and the Monastery had developed the Solanus Casey Center in his honor. We decided to attend Mass at the Capuchins monastery on one particular day, which will be forever in my heart. The Mass was typical, the usual congregation and great priests. I was the only one that seemed out of place during the Mass.

During Mass, we were sitting at the back of the church

when I started to sniffle, then cry, then weep. I was wearing a dark zippered sweatshirt with pockets, my hands were in those pockets, and I kept wiping my face with my hands, had no Kleenex, of course. My sweatshirt was wet with tears. I COULD NOT STOP CRYING, I was so embarrassed, and I couldn't figure out what was wrong with me. I was not melancholy, I was just nonstop crying during the Mass. I felt sorry for Glenn. I was sure everyone was going to think he was a wife abuser or some such thing, although he didn't seem embarrassed. From time to time, he would ask me if I was alright, then put his arm around me, squeezing my shoulder. Occasionally, the people behind me would pat me on the shoulder in a consoling gesture. I would mumble, "Thank you, thanks a lot. I am okay." It was obvious; I had concerned those around me.

> Therefore, as the holy Spirit says; "Oh, that today you would hear his voice, " " Harden not your hearts as at the rebellion in the day of testing in the desert," Hebrews 3:7-8

I had never seen anyone weep like that who didn't have a real problem. It was bewildering. The weeping ceased as abruptly as it began, when Mass was over, the tears stopped. I smiled at those nearby, like, "all is well, nothing to see here." Then, Glenn and I went out in the atrium where Blessed Solanus was entombed. A beautiful room with tall windows, light streaming in, lush green foliage on the outside. We knelt at the rale that surrounded his tomb to pray. There were notes left, and other mementos in this room. We seemed to have knelt there for what seemed a long time. Not feeling strained, or tired, but at peace, embraced by calmness and very content. I was not crying, just recovering from crying. I noticed that Glenn was walking around the room, similar to one walking at an art museum, slow and pondering, into the next room. I finally felt complete and ready to follow him and we continued our exploration of the monastery.

We went to the monastery souvenir shop, which was complete with any treasure you would want to purchase for yourself or family, and we bought many small gifts to take home to our unsuspecting family. It may be terrible to say, but I may judge how much I like experiences by the souvenir shop and the treasures I can bring home to remember it by. In this shop, they were giving out first-hand relics for free; this was unbelievable to me. First degree relics are items that had been physically touched by the blessed person. The saint if you will. These relics were all related to Solanus Casey in some way; many were small pieces of his clothing. Relics contain the power of God and are treasures to have. It seemed there was an unlimited supply of these oval discs with a piece of his clothing on it and a picture of Solanus Casey on the opposite side. I am embarrassed to say how many we brought home that day. We were in love with Blessed Solanus Casey.

When we returned to our church, we shared this experience with Sister Cyrilla, our resident religious sister. That is, my uncontrollable weeping episode at the monastery. As I told her how overcome with weeping I was, she smiled and said, "That was the gift of the Holy Spirit, Tears of the Holy Spirit." I didn't know what she meant at the time, but I was glad there was a name for it. I was reassured that I wasn't any weirder for having a breakdown in Mass. The fruits of the Tears of the holy Spirit are joy and abiding peace. I can honestly say that I still feel like that to this day. I feel blessed and happy every day. Thank you, Lord. I have yet to meet anyone that has had a similar experience, but I know they are out there.

6

PERSONALIZING YOUR LIVING BIBLE

A Bible should be opened, not sitting collecting dust.

When Glenn returned to the Catholic Church, he purchased a Catholic Bible for me. I didn't know there were even such things as Catholic and non-Catholic Bibles. I remember the last Bible I bought at the Episcopal church had seven books of the Apocrypha in it. The priest explained that Apocrypha was not authorized or something, but they wanted to include them because we might see them in other bibles. Yes, the Catholic bible has them all. These so-called apocryphal or deuteronical books are Tobit, Judith, 1 Maccabees, 2 Maccabees, Wisdom of Solomon, Wisdom of Sirach(also called Ecclesiasticus), Baruch including the Letter of Jeremiah and additions to Esther. Now, when I am purchasing a bible or picking up one at an estate sale, I look to see if the bible I pick up has Maccabees and I know it is not only Catholic but complete. There is also an actual section in the front of a Catholic bible that will indicate that the book is authorized by the National Conference of

43

Catholic Bishops. But, back then I didn't know any of that. I was not a biblical scholar, still am not.

The bible that Glenn gave me is beautiful. It is a white leather-bound, large print book. Yes, large print. I am only getting older, and I hate to struggle to read. I want to be able to pick up any book and be able to read, not worry about the lighting or font size or what glasses I am wearing. This book was and is perfect. It is the Saint Joseph Edition of the New American Bible.

We had just started the two-year Discipleship classes at the Catholic church, and one of the first lecturers instructed us to make our Bibles a living family history. She said,-write in it, journal, take notes, make anniversary or historical notations in it. Whatever was important or interesting to me. I'll admit, it seemed very sacrileges at first, but after I got over my 1st scribblings in my bible, it has been my memory. I can look through my bible, and I will see how I have documented my growth in Christ and my life within the pages. It reminds me of some many sweet memories, phrases I liked, scriptures, when kids got new jobs or asked for help, past seminars and the focus of the lecturers, and marriages, births, and funerals of my loved ones. Someday I will pass it down to my daughter as a keepsake of my time here on earth.

We have recently started a new tradition when our grandchildren turn thirteen, to present them with their first adult bible. I pray they will make it their living Bible and when they read it they will be reminded or events in their lives, the miracles, the accomplishments and what they have survived to date with the grace of God.

My Bible has also been instrumental in supporting my

writings for this book. As I leaf through its pages, it reminds me of significant ideas and events that I may have forgotten but has a place in the pages of this book. What were my past concerns, what was I praying over and many times what prayers were answered. It also reminds me of all the good and bad times that have passed over the years and how quickly time does fly.

I have learned the Bible is not the pillar of the Catholic Church. The Church is the pillar of the Catholic faith. The Church is made up of the people. So, in essence, the most important thing in our faith are Gods people and the love He has for us and the love we have for each other. It is easy to forget that we must see Christ in everyone.

> Lord, when did we see you hungry and feed you, or thirsty and give you something to drink? When did we see you a stranger and invite you in, or needing clothes and clothe, you? When did we see you sick or in prison and go to visit you? " The King will reply, Truly I tell you, whatever you did for one of the least of these brothers and sisters of mine, you did for me." Matthew 25:37-40

We are all too guilty of attributing bad intentions to other people's actions. Maligning others allows us to dehumanize them and rationalize our prejudices. In other words, it makes it easier for us not to like them or think less of them.

Road rage is something we can all relate to. It gives us the freedom to "vent" and feel superior. What I tell myself is that I don't know the whole story and I seldom get road rage. If I do, it is probably misplaced anger over something else that I should be directing my anger towards. I try to think maybe, they,(those people that have done me wrong), are on their way to the Emergency Room. How do I know they aren't? I don't know, and I don't presume the worst of them because they interfered with my daydreaming on the road or beat me to a turn. I try to remember to thank God, that I don't have any emergencies to rush off too. Plus, if I am honest, I know that I have probably caused a little road rage in others because of my driving. Have you ever been at a stop sign, looked both ways, twice, then pulled out and when you look in your rear-view mirror you realize you pulled out in front of a car and they are slamming on their breaks behind you? That was probably me; I seem to do this. I have a blind spot for certain color cars it appears. I just don't see them.

My daughter Janice hates to confide in me when it comes to her telling me of an experience she had with someone else and the injustice done to her in some way. I always find the silver lining in the situation or the good side of the instigator. I rarely commiserate with the "offended party." Janice will sigh and say, "Mom it wasn't like that at all, it was a bad thing." I realize this is exasperating to the person confiding in me, but someone has to defend the person, that is not in the room. There are always two sides to the story, and I don't believe that people are intentionally malicious. I think people have different views because of different life experiences or how they were brought up or their lack of education or something which is not entirely their fault. Politics is like this. I don't see either side as totally right or wrong, good or bad. Each side has their reasons and I can listen without letting my emotions control my actions. That will lead nowhere, with no positive results, just alienation. It is similar to when my kids umpired little league. They did the best they could, they weren't professionals, and most of the parents gave them this leeway. The call they made was their perception of the play at that time. That doesn't mean there is not a right and wrong to decisions or the "plays of life." Some will work out better over time or maybe for more people, and I have firm beliefs of what I know is to be right and wrong. I also know that I will change no one's mind by yelling or forcing my opinions on them. Gods way is best, showing love, kindness and the mercy of God is what it takes to change hearts and minds.

Over the years I know my views have changed. The more one learns the more one changes their decision-making skills. It is all about what skills we have in our so-called toolbox of life.

This ability to not condemn others or put them down helped me be a more compassionate nurse. Or maybe it was my education as a nurse helped form my ability to be nonjudgmental to others. Either way, seeing Christ in others can be done. Now, let me say that being nonjudgmental does not mean I don't have opinions or won't try to change someone's mind if I think they are doing something morally wrong. It is our responsibility as Christians to be role models. Good role models. To help form and guide, influence and change the direction of others who may be headed down a path that is not going to be truthful or keep them out of trouble. In the raising of seven children, I have come to understand that just because I say something, and people agree it does not mean there will be any action that follows. Often a positive response from others is a method of getting me to stop talking, or they may say "preaching" about something. I probably do the same thing. I have a phrase I use to agree but not agree, and it is, "I can see why you feel that way." Or even, " Wow." I hate them used on me, so it is really in rare circumstances where I am trapped in a monologue by someone because I try to be a good listener. Generally, I try to listen to what is being told to me, what they are saying means something to the other person.

I have to tell you about the coffee table Bible we had. You may have seen the large pictorial type, that is about three inches thick and a foot long. This bible must have been a wedding present or something of significance, because we had it sitting out all the time on the coffee table. I asked Glenn if we couldn't put it away since we didn't use it. It was just collecting dust and was heavy to move. It seemed to take up more room on the table than it needed. I will never forget what Glenn said, "No. I may not open it much, but it reminds me every day when I walk by it what I should be doing. It stays." I have never forgotten that lesson.

So, the final answer is," Get a Bible and make it your living Bible." Do not be afraid of writing in the margins, underlining significant scriptures and adding dates and names. I have a lot of autographs in front of it by speakers or priests that I have gained insight from. Some have passed on now, but I have their signature and my memory of them. As you write you will find your Bible becomes something that is not left on the shelf or kept neat and tidy but is handy in your bag or at your morning reading table or going to all those seminars with you. Soon your Bible will look like you open the pages, often. It may not be pristine, but neither is our life. Remember our faith is in our hearts and our Church. Our Bibles support this faith; it is not the only source of our faith. Our faith was not written down for over 400 years; very few people were literate. There was no printing press until the 1400s. The Christian faith was handed down by sacred tradition and was oral. Then the various books or canons of the Bible were put together to complete what we now know as the Bible. Once this bible was bound together, the Monks would painstakingly copy it for churches, but it was very rare to have a copy. If there was one at a church it was often chained to the altar, so it was available but could not be stolen. They could not get them replaced. I hear the Bible is still a number one best seller and the most sold book in the world. That in itself is comforting.

7

THE REAL PRESENCE OF JESUS

Be still and know that I am your God

My mom was raised in the Catholic church and then converted to Episcopal after her marriage. Looking back, it appears she always replicated her Catholic faith in the Episcopal church. We learned to genuflect, we believed that the Eucharist was the body and blood of Christ, we had one Baptism, we didn't have Confession, but the priest liked to talk privately with you one on one annually, and we went to church every Sunday. When I converted to Catholicism, it was not that big of a stretch for me. The service itself is conducted in the same way, but I felt it had more meaning in the Catholic church. Bless my dad, and I know why he said, "We have all that, you don't need to change churches!" For his part, he did have it all. For me, I needed more of my faith and less of agreeing with the morals of the secular world. As a friend from my Catholic church would say, "We have more stuff than any other church." I will always be learning more stuff about the Catholic faith. It seems endless, and I am not surprised that I can't recall all I have already learned. I seem to like "stuff."

At one time, at least for the first 1500 years after Christ, there was only one Christian church, Catholic. Catholic means universal, and it encompassed everyone. Everything Christian was Catholic. I always find it amusing when some people will say they are, "Christian," but not think of a Catholic as a Christian. Catholics are the "original" Christians. At the time of Christ, there were Pagans, Christians, Judeans, Various Gods and Goddess's, Astrologist and Cults. Protestantism didn't come along for another 1500 years when King Henry the VIII split off from Pope and the Roman Catholic Church and started the Church of England in the 1530's. That decision changed the apostolic succession of the two churches. The Roman Catholic church kept on following the line of Peter the original Pope and the Church of England proceeded with the Archbishop of Canterbury as its head. For Catholics, without the apostolic succession the Mass would not be legitimate. The direct line from Christ must be there.

When the Mass is celebrated we believe that the bread and wine are transformed into the body and blood of Christ, this belief in the transformation was brought home to me when I was still going to both Catholic and Episcopal churches. The Episcopal priest at the time, seemed to cavalierly throw Jesus down on the altar, the "bread". That is how it appeared to me. I remember how horrified I was that he did not treat the Blessed Host with reverence. I knew I could no longer consume the host at the Episcopal church. Now, it may have only been that priest or that particular host. I have never forgotten it, and that realization became one of those turning points in my spiritual journey.

The Eucharist is not a remembrance, not a memory of what occurred. The Eucharist is a participation in the body and blood of Christ.

> The cup of blessing that we bless is it not a participation in the blood of Christ? The bread that we break is it not a participation in the body of Christ? 1 Corinthians 10:16

There is a red globe in the altar area of all Catholic churches with the candle lit in it which indicates that Jesus is present in the Tabernacle at the altar. When we enter our pews or cross in front of the altar or tabernacle, we will genuflect and make the sign of the cross. We are genuflecting to Jesus. We are not genuflecting to a cross, a light, a location or a symbol. We are genuflecting to Jesus who is in the Tabernacle. This light is always lit when Jesus is present in the tabernacle and confirms this for us. The candle is only extinguished when there are no Blessed hosts at the altar.

What is comforting about the Catholic church is that it is the same around the world: the same readings, Gospel, liturgy, the order of Mass. One doesn't have to speak the local language to attend and understand the service. On special High Masses, the service will be in Latin. Not all understand Latin of course, but we all know what they are saying by where we are in the liturgy. There is a hymn we sing called, "All are Welcome". It could be the motto of our Catholic faith, there are no exclusions and we mean it. Mass is Mass, anywhere, anytime.

During Advent or Lent we will pray in Latin more often

especially the Holy, Holy or Our Father and it is beautiful. Conveniently, we have little cards in the pews with the words in Latin. Another thing you will find in the pews is a paperback book called the Missalette. The missalette includes all of the daily and Sunday readings, psalms, special prayers, Order of Mass and many other useful, service cues for the current three months. No one has to be confused when attending Mass for the first time. Everyone uses this book to read along, even folks that attend every day. The Catholic church has a three-year cycle of rotation for scripture readings, and when that is complete, basically the whole Bible has been read. So, Yes, Catholics do read the bible; we can hear scripture every day or read it at home. Then we are so fortunate to have a homily or sermon which is always a breaking of the word of God by the Priest or Deacon. The difference I have noted between any Catholic church and the non-Catholic churches that I have attended is that our homilies are not a political or social speech, but are directed at the Gospel of the day and the interpretation of it as it can apply to our week. Now, I have heard others say that their preachers were motivational or speaking on topics, like child discipline or financial management or whatever the secular feel-good message is for the day. I understand that those speeches are necessary and helpful. But, when one listens to the Word of God, He also lays out how to raise your children, treat your elders, manage your money, treat one another. God is the originator of motivation. He led Moses, a man who did not want to speak in public or was someone who didn't think he could. Moses became a great leader. God changed the heart of Saul to stop tormenting Christians into a defender of Christians and Jesus, He took illiterate fisherman and made them fishers of men, willing to give up homes and families to follow Him. That is motivation.

The inside of the Catholic Churches will be similar too. They are designed to create an atmosphere of Heaven on Earth. The front and center is the altar with Jesus on a crucifix. There will be a crucified statue of Jesus, bigger than life on the wall or suspended from the ceiling. On either side of him will be the Saints. Usually, the Blessed Virgin Mary is on the left of the altar and His Foster Father, St. Joseph is on the right side of the altar. The stained-glass windows will depict Saints, Sacraments and Feast Days. The use of incense is to make one think of the sky and heaven. All of the color from the stained glass, the figures in statues or pictures and music are to enhance the Mass and represent the time, talent and money that people have provided to add beauty to the worship space and make a fit place for God. Our churches are not unadorned town halls or gathering places, but sites of worship. The worship of God, it should be a space fit for God.

The priest himself is dressed up, wearing vestments. There are several layers to what he wears, and they all have a rational, which is beyond me to remember. He does not appear like any ordinary person in the congregation. He is the Shepherd of the congregation. His vestments are to depict shepherd's robe or clothing during Jesus' time. The colors of his vestments will change during different liturgical seasons; they are Advent or Christmas(purple), Ordinary Time(after Epiphany), Lent and Easter.

Speaking of dressing up, if you attend many Catholic churches the last two weeks of Lent, you will not see crucifixes or statues. They will be shrouded in purple cloth(Lenten color). Now, this is not a requirement, but since the 1700s, this practice has been done. To me, it is a visible signal that we as parishioners have two weeks left to complete what we promised or start our good intentions. It is the sprint to the finish. Most people give up things for Lent, but in the Catholic church, it is not always giving things we like up, like chocolate or TV as a penance but adding good things that engage us or grow our spiritual life. Other additions could be, going to daily Mass, or giving to a charity, or starting a bible study, or writing a book of your faith journey, hmm. Something that helps you to focus more on God and less on your wants and desires.

There have been many great educational offerings this Lent and sad to say; I haven't made time to go. We have had Lenten breakfast, lunches, and suppers. Everyone has heard of the Catholic Fish Dinners on Fridays. During Lent, Catholics are to either abstain from meat; chicken, beef, lamb, pork and turkey on Fridays or you can add a personal penance on Fridays like reading the bible or praying the rosary. Those don't seem like penances, but they would be something you don't normally do. So, you have sacrificed your time to do something for God and ultimately yourself. Glenn and I prefer to keep meatless Friday's year-round, it is almost "hip" these days. But we are far from, "hip", you would know that if you knew us. I once described myself as eclectic, to my daughter Janice and her friend Jackie and they laughed and said, "No, you are just weird and old-fashioned". No meat Fridays are a good penance year-round, hardly a hardship. It also gives me the opportunity to serve more plant-based menus they are tasty, and it gives me a change up from preparing meals around a meat protein. Just saying the phrase "plant based", is new to me. What is wrong with meatless or vegetarian? We like breakfast foods for supper or bean soups and a favorite would be grilled cheese sandwich. It lessens the common questions of "What's for dinner?" meal planning. Have to love that!

Speaking of penances, they are not to be confused with sacrifices. God does not need or want our sacrifices. No sacrifice that we could offer would be enough for our sins. Only God could produce a sacrifice that would cover all of our past, present, and future sins. God did this through his Son, Jesus Christ. The last sacrifice was Jesus, and God expects no more. That sacrifice cannot be topped.

Before Jesus, the people sacrificed all sorts of animals, calves, goats, lambs, pigeons. I am not sure what animal is smaller than a bird, that they may have used it. Often, if they couldn't afford an animal, they would use grain. Sacrifices were the thing to please God before Jesus, in the Old Testament. Now, we live according to the New Testament and the Gospels of Jesus. We cannot always read something in the Old Testament and apply it to today's standards. Before Christ, the people lived by rules and guidelines, the Commandments. They didn't have a savior. Rules kept them in line and out of bedlam and chaos. We now have a savior, which encompasses, His words, deeds, and actions are to teach us. We are in the New Covenant, a promise with God.

Our marriages are celebrated in this Covenant. We don't marry only a spouse, but we marry into a promise with God to uphold and support this promise of marriage. The covenant is another reason we don't take marriage lightly. To be married in the Catholic church, one must be speaking to a Priest no less than six months before the intended date of matrimony and attend marriage preparation and a weekend retreat with other engaged couples. We want marriages to last and not be entered into under the disclaimer that, "We can always get divorced if it doesn't work out." Now, I know that begs that question, " But, there is divorce in Catholic churches, right?". No, not really. But, before I speak to divorce, let me state the requirements for marriage.

First, you both have to agree and be free without impediment to marriage. An impediment could include being old enough, not being already married, ability to understand it is a marriage, you will be of different genders, and agree to accept children and raise them in the Catholic faith.

Second, the couple must have the intention of wanting to be married and give their consent. No coercion to become married and that they want to be faithful to each other.

Third, the couple must follow the sacrament of marriage faithfully in the marriage ceremony. In other words, we don't have ad lib vows.

To a non-Catholic, these rules may sound pretty stiff, but successful marriages are planned and cultivated, they don't just happen. There must be an agreement to what the marriage entails, and public support of the married couple is also essential.

Now, on to divorce. We don't call it divorce; we don't believe in divorce. The Catholic church can have your previous marriage annulled if it meets prescribed guidelines. This would make your previous marriage appear like it did not happen. Marriage annulment is completed for everyone that wants to enter the Catholic church or to marry in the Catholic church.

When Glenn and I married, we were both divorced at the

time. We filled out the annulment paperwork, which included witness statements from two or three other people. We had to indicate where we were married the first time and whether it was a valid marriage. It is quite lengthy. It can take couples a year or two to complete the process. Then a formal decision is made after a review of all information. We were fortunate that neither of us had been married as a Catholic the first time, and our annulments took only months to complete. The Church will not annul valid marriages, because they are a covenant with God. There are about four basic reasons for an annulment, and if one of them is broken by a spouse, an annulment may be attained after inquiry decision. The rules for marital annulment are much more complex than what I have stated, but in a nutshell, this is what they are;

First, there wasn't a clear understanding that marriage was taking place. This lack of awareness could be related to mental illness or lack of consciousness. We never drink alcohol on the day of the wedding until after the ceremony at the reception, and this is the reason.

Second, a psychological condition, including substance or alcohol abuse.

Third, an error of person or quality of the person, you married the wrong person, for example, a mail order bride, or adultery, an arrest record, a medical disease, or lack religious conviction.

Fourth, you married and found out your spouse did not want children, or just married you for reasons of convenience, for example, a Green Card.

You can see why it takes a formal process to sort this all out — one other thing. When marriages are annulled, it does not make children from that marriage illegitimate. I have heard this said, and it is not accurate.

Whew! I hadn't planned on going down that road, but it occurred to me and I wanted to share what we do in the Catholic Church. Especially, how it has affected my conversion and take the mystery and confusion out of what many think are our Catholic rules. Our "rules" are meant to keep us all on the track to salvation. It is so easy to get detoured on this earth and have to stumble back through trial and error to the right road. The sacrament of Marriage is one of the most important for your everyday life. The annulment of a sacrament should require considerable consideration.

We live in such a disposable world. Where everything is discarded with Friday's trash pick-up, has an expiration date or no longer fits our lifestyles. We can't let our faith fall into that category. I don't know who coined the phrase, "The grass is always greener on the other side of the fence," but they knew what they were referring to. It is just a perception. I say, "Fertilize your own grass,! people." If we spent more time nurturing our own backyards rather than gazing at what others have and thinking they live the perfect life, OURS would be perfect. Having old, comfortable things, relationships and living faith is a safety net. You know that feeling when you have been traveling and yearn to go home because you are homesick? You miss your dogs, your bed and your everyday food? Well, that can be your faith, your quiet time with the One that totally, "gets you." The person that needs no explanations, no subterfuge and accepts and knows all the good and bad of your life and will love you unconditionally.

How do we become closer to God? One way is to perform some a penance. When we do any penance, it strengthens our will to say "No," to sin. Let's say, I want an iced coffee. If I give in to this urge every time I pass McDonald's it makes me weaker, physically and spiritually. I will feel like I have no control over my decision. But, if just once, I drive by McDonald's and don't stop to get an iced coffee, then the next time it will be easier to drive by. It gets easier and easier, and that is penance. Penance makes us stronger. When we give up something, give it up in the name of God. You will see the difference.

8

FREQUENTLY ASKED
QUESTIONS(FAQ)

What's all the buzz about?

N ow, let me answer some frequently asked questions (FAQ) that are on your mind about Catholics, and I will try to lay them to rest. We are not that weird or mysterious.

Do Catholics dance? Yes, we do — no problem with that.

Do Catholics gamble? Yes, we do. We have church bingo parties, card parties, casino nights and the money earned goes to a church project. We are not forbidden from gambling elsewhere either but let's put it in perspective. Don't get over your head that would be a sin.

Do Catholics drink alcohol? Yes, we do. We use real wine during the Eucharist, no grape juice. We may celebrate at parties with spirits, and we sell alcohol at casino night. Maybe it's a donation and not a sale, not sure, liquor laws and all those rules. This is all done moderately but let's be honest. We are not the No! No! The church you thought we might be.

Why is a priest celibate? Jesus was, and that is their model for leading the flock. Leading a parish is a time-consuming job, and if the priests time and attention were divided between family concerns and his parish concerns, one would be shortchanged. The parish family is the priest's family, and the church is his home. I know you will have heard of a priest that has children, the reason for that could be, some men become a priest after they have had a family, and their wife has died. This is may be acceptable. They then devote their lives to God and the church. They are also celibate at this point. They cannot remarry once they take Holy Orders. This goes for the Deacon who has had a wife pass on too. A Deacon is not to remarry if their wife should die, and he is to remain celibate. Men often become Deacon's while married and receive their Holy Orders.

Do you have any female priests? No, we do not. It may be as simple as Jesus chose only men as disciples. When Jesus washed the disciple's feet as a demonstration of servitude to others, He did this to the apostles only. Then again, at the Last Supper when Jesus broke bread with the Apostles, it was only men. Jesus is the bridegroom of the Church. The Church is the bride of Christ.

Women are not to be disparaged, however. Women have always been complimentary to men. If you have a successful, happy marriage, it is due in part to the complimentary nature of men and women. Women in the Catholic church are very important and hold leadership roles. God also gave women the precious gift of carrying children. A man can never truly understand maternal feelings, instincts that come from this early union with our child. We are so important in the upbringing in a way that is different than the men's modeling. I realize that men and women are more versed in replicating each other's' roles in modern culture, but when we are honest, we can site so many beneficial differences in men and women. These differences are crucial and fundamental in our emotional health. I like to site the differences in how many and women usually shop. It goes back to the hunting and gathering history of mankind, I think. Men have targets, hunt for what they want and take it home. Women gather and look and meander and select by comparison before they put things in their carts. I love when Glenn goes with me because he helps me carry things, yet I know he is holding back a lot of signs and, "Why do we need that?" type questions, to not ruin "my" shopping enjoyment. For my part, when we go to Lowe's, I say, " I will wait in the car."

Does the Catholic church tell you what to do with your finances? Nope. Like every church, we have projects that we are asked to prayerfully consider donating to or the Annual Bishops Appeal that as a community we want to support. Then there is our church financial interest. We all receive an annual expense report from the financial officer of the church, showing what the church spends, salaries, where all the monies go and where we are short of cash, very transparent. Do we get phone calls or visits from members of the church to ask us to increase our giving? Nope. We believe all are parishioners are adults and can determine this amount through prayer. We also trust in the strength of the Holy Spirit and his ability to move through the hearts and minds of the Church faithful to obtain what is in the best interest of the Church. The Catholic church is one of the most generous churches in the world. Catholic

Charities provides monies worldwide as do Catholic Relief services.

> Each must do as already determined, without sadness or compulsion, for God loves a cheerful giver. 2 Corinthians 9: 7

What about, cohabitation or premarital sex? Both are common in secular society but the Church? Ouch! Nope, those are not approved. Cohabitation and premarital sex are both outsides of marriage and may produce children which further adds to complexity to your life.

> God blessed them, saying: "Be fertile and multiply; fill the earth and subdue it. Genesis 1:28

If you notice He blessed them as in our marriage covenant before he told them to be fertile. He also talks of this in Genesis, the beginning of the Bible. Doesn't that in itself seem significant? I think He understood human nature and wanted to lay down the ground rules from the get-go.

Do you allow homosexuals in your church? Yes, and heterosexuals. We do not approve of premarital sex in any relationship. Do we judge single people, No. What individuals do is between them and God. It is not for parishioners to comment on or cast aspirations about. The same thing goes for what we wear at Mass. You should always wear clothing that does not draw attention and distract people from prayer or focusing on Jesus. That is why you will not see, shoulders exposed or short shorts, or in some churches open toed sandals. These small "t" traditions vary from church to church and are not written in stone.

We live or try to live by the Ten Commandments and Biblical scripture, and we have a book called the Catechism of the Catholic Church that explains, defines and tells us where to get the answers to all questions Catholic. If I ever want to know the Church's teaching in a pinch, I will look it up.

> Let marriage be honored among all and the marriage bed
> be kept undefiled, for God will judge the immoral and
> adulterers. Hebrews 13: 4

Does the Catholic church frown on birth control? Yes, they do more than frown. It is a sin to use artificial or mechanical birth control measures. We believe that we are in control of the size of our families by being connected to God. Before cohabitation was so prevalent, people would wait until they married to have sex which lessened the number of children as did waiting to marry until you married and could support a wife. When one is living outside God's plan, it has a snowball effect on increased children it seems. Premarital sex can lead to birth control or abortion or marriage to possibly the wrong person. These are all stages of life that do not benefit us in the long run. We must be smarter than that and think more of ourselves and why God has plans for mankind that do not include that sequence of events. The Catholic Church has a program to educate couples on how to avoid or delay pregnancies. This technique is called Natural Family Planning. I have heard, it is very doable. It was before my time as a Catholic, and so I never learned how to do that. I always found that family economics limited family size. One of the funniest most fun memories is when we told our oldest five kids that we were having another baby. That would be our seventh child. My oldest daughter, Ang, maybe I should say, my oldest princess, started to wale and cried, "NO! Now I will never get anything new. We can't afford it!". To this day, she will tell you our littlest babies "made" her life complete and blessed. God always knows best.

The Catholic church has three vocations that they consider God-given. The vocation of being single, married and this would be a faithful love in the Sacrament of Marriage or of being called to the priesthood, and religious life. The Church will help individuals discern what they are called to do as a vocation and find the natural contentment that comes from being in the right place at the right time. A vocation that God has called them to live. If you are wondering about same-sex attractions, there are support groups for that too. One such group is called the Courage Apostolates, and then the group for family members is called Encourage. They can be found online and shared. We are about the love of God and helping people, not judging. Everyone is working through something and only with the help of others and God's grace can we get to where we need to go.

The Vocation Prayer that we pray before all Masses.

VOCATION PRAYER

*Lord Jesus, Son of the Eternal Father, and
Mary Immaculate,*

Give to our young people and single adults,
the generosity necessary
To follow Your call to their vocation in life.
Give to parents that faith, love, and spirit of
sacrifice, which will inspire them
to offer their children to God's service, and to
rejoice whenever one of their children
is a call to the priesthood, the religious life,
or faithful love in the Sacrament of
Marriage.
Let your example, and that of our Blessed
Mother and St. Joseph,
Encourage both young people and parents,
and let Your grace sustain them. Amen.

I looked up the chronology of the beginning of the most common faiths and found it fascinating and will share it here. One thing I want to make clear is that I am happy whenever anyone is going to church, any church. I believe that faith is a journey which often starts with, "I don't believe" or "I don't think I believe." But am open to God". Anywhere you are comfortable, get on board.

32AD Catholicism 1521 Lutherism 1534 Anglican Church of England

1537 Mennonites 1582 Congregationalism 1607 Episcopal Church in the USA

1609 Baptist 1648 Quakers 1693 Amish

1738 Methodism 1830 Mormons 1840 Seventh Day Adventist

1845 Southern Baptist 1870 Jehovah Witness 1960 Charismatic Non-denominational

1968 United Methodist 20th century Pentecostal

I pray that someday all of our journeys will lead to the biblical scripture that Paul wrote;

One body and one Spirit, as you were also Lord, one faith, one baptism; one God and Father of all, which is over all and through all and in all. Ephesians 4:4

9

HOME PRAYER ROOMS

We call it the den, but it is so much more.

We have an open room adjacent to the upstairs stairway on the way to our bedroom, and we converted it to our spiritual place. We were lucky to purchase a rectangular table for $25.00 which we use as the altar. Once we put the candles, the crucifix and the incense on it, there was no doubting what it was. It sometimes has too much sitting on it, with the Virgin Mary on one end and St Joseph on the other and then the occasional Pope picture. I know my husband dislikes a cluttered altar, so I try to maintain it, but...

We call this room the den because when we first started calling it the prayer room, the non-Catholics in the family were a little put-off and seemed to be repelled by all of the "idolatry." We have since either straightened out that concept or maybe just desensitized them. We still had two High School kids at home when Glenn returned to the church and they were very happy in the Episcopal church. Why wouldn't they be? It is a nice church. But, when your parents change churches, you all change.

As I have learned it is a calling by the Holy Spirit to come, not just a choice one makes to join the Catholic church. The kids were confused and perhaps a little over-whelmed by the crucifixes on the wall and the change to our "den." One of our older daughters, Janice, lamented, "Why now? I am attending the healing prayer group at the Epis-copal church and feel good there." We reassured her that this was our journey, not hers and she would know if she ever needed to change. Little did she know at the time, that the man she was going steady with was a Catholic and was soon going to become the active Catholic he is today.

Janice was a support to me when I wanted to learn more about becoming a Catholic. I had signed up for a class by Father Farrell in Kalamazoo, called, "Catholicism for Dummies." I figured that was me. Janice didn't know anything about being a Catholic either but was willing to check these classes out with me. So, for several weeks we drove over to Kalamazoo and learned what the big deal was. The classes took much of the fear and confusion out of conversion, and we both decided we could pursue classes to become Catholic and joined different home town parishes on the same Easter Vigil on March 22, 2018. All converts join the Catholic church on the night of the Easter Vigil. This night ends a process that converts to thru to determine if Catholicism is right for them. about nine months of weekly education and questioning about what Catholicism is. All components of the catholic faith are discussed so we can all truly be in one communion when we are at the Eucharistic table. These classes are called the Rite of Christian Initiation of Adults (RCIA).

The date of Easter changes with every calendar year, and it can be as early as March 22 or as late as April 25th. The date is determined by the paschal full moon date. The Paschal full moon is the first full moon after the ecclesiastical full moon date following March 20th. That is probably too much information, but that is a question I have had. When I joined the church, I had to remember the date for that year, since it changes every year. I converted to Catholicism on March 22, 2018 and Glenn was my sponsor. A sponsor is a Catholic that attends all of the RCIA classes with you and is on hand to answer questions and stand with you as you join the Catholic faith and is an active Catholic themselves.

Our den has changed over the years from bearing all of the Stations of the Cross on the walls to only a couple of large pictures from Hobby Lobby of the Nativity or the Last Supper. It has transitioned again to be more of a Blessed Mary, Virgin Mary, Perpetual Help Mary, Miraculous Mary, site. I have obtained some beautiful used prints, and paintings at estate sales, Goodwill and auctions. Sad to say but religious art is not in demand. Most of my paintings were $5.00. I understand that everyone may not want a two foot by an eighteen-inch framed print of the Blessed Virgin in their homes, but I love them.

We have this flea market type auction near us, and I have picked up bags of religious medals, some with relics in them and old rosaries. What treasures! I feel it is such an honor to care for them. I know at one time they were cherished, used and blessed. I feel compelled to buy them at these auctions so that they will have a home. A final home that will love them. I have twelve rosaries that I have cleaned hanging from a standing lamp right now; I must move them out of the living room. The grandkids will then want to wear them, and my folks will be trying to avoid looking at them, so the rosaries must at least leave the living room. God love them. I don't have any little pouches for them, but I will find an appropriate place for them. When I have my family over for parties, there are about forty people invited over to my 960 sq. ft house. You can imagine the logistics of that. I can usually manage to set up tables for all and then I pray for a sunny day, so the kids will go outside.

The prayer room is used for the Liturgy of the Hours in the morning or just reading or praying. My husband made two priediux's or kneelers, for us to kneel on and they are on either side of the altar. I have to admit, I am not that comfortable kneeling in them, but they are gorgeous. I have a three-foot-tall cement-like Samaritan Woman, the Woman at the Well. My granddaughter can be head to head with her. This cement woman reminds me of who I once was, how I was forgiven, guided and loved. I can't pass her without touching her head and thinking, "Thank you." We all have some of the unforgiven in us and think we are too unworthy for God's grace. But, so untrue. There is nothing God cannot forgive; he is all love and mercy.

> At that moment his disciples returned , and were amazed that he was talking with a woman, but still no one said, " Why are you talking with her?" The woman left her water jar and went into the town and said to the people, "Come

see a man who told me everything I have done. Could he possibly be the Messiah?" John 4: 27-29

Another change in the room is that the windows have pseudo-stained-glass panels over them, of God and Jesus. Glenn was in a passion for creating stain glass and made them for many windows in the house. At least the bottom half of the double hung windows. They are lovely. I even have one of colorful peacocks in the bathroom. We have given our daughters Janice and Gabrielle each a stained glass with electric lights in them to hang on their walls. The stained glass cast bright colors across the floor in the sunlight. At night or early morning when you drive by the house, and a light is left on in the prayer room, the windows are very colorful viewing them from the outside in.

So, really, does it look like a den? I think everyone has just gotten used to our Catholic quirkiness. I say live your faith and others will be reminded of theirs.

LET THE CHILDREN COME

The "Real" superheroes are in the Bible

We are blessed to have fourteen grandchildren with the fifteenth is arriving this July. We will have five grandboys and ten grandgirls. It is not a cliché that grandchildren are the best. Not that we didn't enjoy our children, but we aren't as responsible for the grandchildren. Just love and hugs. Since we both retired, we can spend some quality time with them. I regret that I couldn't do this when we worked full-time, but, we were just too tired at the end of the day. So, we missed a lot of the cute stages with the older grandkids. We saw everyone at family gatherings and birthdays, but the amount of time you get with any one person is so limited and distracting that there is no quality to it. It just about keeps you on a face recognition basis. I find it is especially busy when hosting. You are always, prepping, preparing or managing the party. Some of my older girls' favorite times with me are the party autopsies afterward. We discuss what everyone talked about or heard. It is amazing how many different things you can learn when you pool your conversations, so fun. I don't think I consider that gossip. We have a family that we share most things unless you tell us not too. The boys know if you tell one sister, the rest will know, and or someone will tell mom. It has its good and bad sides, but on the whole, it keeps us all close and caring. Of course, for those that want a private life, it drives them bonkers, and they are always feeling betrayed. Which is never good if someone's feelings are hurt. That can last months, and it has lasted years. Praise God we have the mercy of Christ and the faith of our fathers that eventually bring everyone around to healing and resolution.

And forgive us our debts, as we also have forgiven our debtors. Mathew 6:12

Then Peter came to Jesus and asked, " Lord, how many times shall I forgive my brother or sister who sins against me? Up to seven times?" Jesus answered, " I tell you, not seven times, but seventy-seven times." Matthew 18: 21-22

I always think of forgiveness as something I have to do, or I won't get into Heaven. My belief is whatever I hold against someone will be held against me. I envision St. Peter, stopping me at the proverbial Pearly Gates and saying, "Remember Christine, when you didn't say you were sorry to so and so? Well, it's too late now. You can't come in. You had your chance when you were on earth." Now, that scares me to death. To not have a chance at eternal life because of my own stubbornness or lack of humility. So that I can live a life of no or close to no regrets, I often tell myself." In five years; will it matter?" Most things will not matter in the next month, let alone a year or five years. So, I don't hold grudges, I am not bitter, nor do I hate anyone. It is a much more comfortable, less stressful way to live if I don't have to cross the street when some particular person is coming towards me that I am trying to avoid.

In my work life if I ran across people that would make me nervous or afraid, or even feel small and I would go out of my way to befriend them or make conversation with them. I found they usually became good friends because I didn't ignore them. My work life would be more relaxed, and my everyday encounters were less fearful. I had a position in which I was in the Directors meeting daily, at the Veterans Hospital explaining my department. My department encompassed a relatively new scope of practice called Telehealth, and no one understood it but the computer geeks, because it was providing healthcare through different location via computer, not face to face in an office. The computer staff at least knew the mechanics of the operation and what to do when the remote site was not operational. It was my job as the Registered Nurse that coordinated the program to encourage the use of this type of new technology in healthcare delivery. Me! Who could barely use the remote control? If I didn't have a husband or son around, the remotes in our house were left untouched, let alone trying to record, or use the computer. It was not my thing; I was back in the word processor era. In case you are wondering why I was in that position, it was not because I applied. I remember, I took a vacation and when I returned management said they had some, "Exciting news for me." They wanted me to lead this new position. It was apparent they chose someone that was not in the room when decisions were made to defend themselves and had a track record of agreeing to do unpleasant tasks that no one else would. This new position I think was part of the impetus into my faith growth.

I was frightened every day of the awesomeness and expanse of the growing department and how the buck stopped at my desk. Thanks be to God, everyone was willing to share their expertise and were as motivated as I was to make the program work. I would pray every morning or before hard tasks that I would have the knowledge, strength, and abilities to do the right thing and be able to explain it to others. The program was eventually a success, but it was through talking to people and acknowledging our learning needs together. Boy, can I digress from grandchildren? I think I was implying not to hold grudges and be like children when it comes to your relationships with others. Like my granddaughter, Ziah who is two will say, "Hug, Hug?"

Ziah saying, "Hug" is something I may have missed when I worked, but now that I see her several times a week, she knows and loves me. She and her sister Joysa, can't wait to come over. I think it has something to do with their love for our dogs, Teddy and Louie. But they know I have the "powpows," (pop cycles). Joysa is four and old enough to behave in church. We take her to adoration quite often. She usually tells me how the bible stories go. "Grandma, what is the Kings name?" me, - I don't know. Joysa, "Pharaoh!" " Grandma, who is Pharaoh to Moses?" me, "I don't remember." "Grandma! his brother! "She could tell you about all of the plagues and don't get her started on the Joseph story with the coat of many colors. She will continuously correct the little details. I have learned not to use these as stories before taking a nap or going to bed. They don't make her tired, they make her hyperalert for errors in my storytelling. Now, the game before naps is – Who can fall asleep first? She is very competitive. It is usually Louie, then grandpa, then Joysa, then me. That works great.

What is remarkable to me is she doesn't go to church often, is not Catholic but her mother is a firm evangelical. The stories they read to them are often biblical. Joysa, says grace before every meal at our house. She makes the Sign of the Cross at our church and prays. I can hear her pray, "I am sorry for hitting Ziah and will do better." I wish I had raised my children with this spirit of Christ at such a young age. I think that is our best hope for faith. They are teaching children when they are young and sponge-like. They love mystery and miracles and magical events. They can tell you the Superheroes of today's cartoons, their names and recite their special powers. But, what we don't share with them enough is that the bible is full of superheroes and villains and that Jesus has the most significant strengths and is the boss of everyone. Kids would love that.

My mom would take us to church every Sunday in Port Huron when we were little. At the end of the year, we would all get a unique pin that looked like a ladder. Each year of not missing any church school on Sunday would be rewarded with the year of the success. We had a ladder that had 5-8 rungs on it. We were always proud of that. Parents that try to get their kids interested in church at twelve or thirteen to help teach them had probably lost the battle before they started. The right choices begin when they are two years old, not when they are in middle school facing peer pressure. No one should be surprised when they don't want anything to do with Jesus or the church at that point. They have developed their mind and opinions without anyone's help but TV, friends or Social Media via the phone. Who knows what they have seen. I pray that my grandchildren all get more exposure to Jesus and his teachings. I pray all the time that my kids and everyone else is called back to church and the love and mercy of Christ. The joy and comfort that comes in a relationship with Him and to learn and know the superheroes we have in the Saints of the Church.

LET THERE BE LIFE

Accepting that we are not God

One of the problems I see with people is that we think we are smarter than God. We tend to believe that we are the only ones that hold all of the facts or know how we will be affected by our decisions and we want to use our free will to make our own decisions without anyone else's help. I know this to be true in the raising of seven children. When as parents we think they are asking for our guidance and advice, it is their subtle way of making us feel important and then getting to the crux of the matter. Often, the bottom line, money. The belief that a little cash and quick change in circumstances can make the most significant positive difference rather than working the problem, paying the dues and putting a little backbone to the grindstone.

Young adults don't seem to learn from their parents' mistakes or the retelling of those mistakes. It is almost a competition for our kids to make the same mistakes as parents but get out of it with less consequence. In today's world, the consequences are worse for doing less. You can try to tell them, that their strategy is sure to backfire, but they won't believe you. I do not remember trying to outdo my parents in the wrong way. I was too afraid of them. Maybe, fear is not the right emotion; I didn't want to let them down. Their approval meant more to me than risking a bad decision. I may not have been a typical '70's child. I was the middle child, a peacemaker, so I didn't rock the boat.

My dad comes from a long line of talkers, folk that can explain in detail and with accuracy any question you might have asked them. He could talk about any subject for fifteen minutes; conversations were not quick. You didn't ask him for anything, especially money. They saw that as a weakness in others if you had to ask for money. They grew up in an era where money was almost non-existent, all things were fixed and passed on, or you went without. They didn't spend extra money on themselves; they didn't have it to pay others when they made stupid mistakes. Unfortunately, Glenn and I always thought we were helping out. I think they call it enabling now. Enabling seems to be a trend that started with the baby boomers when raising their kids.

My parents were not my friends, they were my parents. They were people I did not tell everything too, that I kept secrets from, and pretended I was better than I was, for them. I guess, I thought when our kids would come to us, and we would give them such sound advice they would be grateful and put our counsel to good use, not just make promises never to do it again. Promises that were always one decision or one day away from being broken. There were frequent, "I told you so" moments while raising our kids. Hallmark should have coined an "I told you so" card by now; it happens so often.

This concept of the easy fix is the way I think the killing the life of an unborn or terminating the life of an older adult or infirm person has come to fruition. The "me" generations concept of "I am first" or "I am more important than others" is a factor in what leads us astray in making horrible life-altering decisions for the vulnerable that cannot be reversed. We cannot determine the quality of life of another human being or project what quality of life is onto others. God must determine that. As the saying goes, "I brought you into this world, and I will take you out!". That isn't just a mafia saying, but one in which God could be speaking, only He knows the hour time of our departure.

You know the number of his months; you have fixed the limit which he cannot pass. Job 14:5

I love that there are so many places in the Bible that spell out that God knew us in the womb before we knew we were pregnant, and he entrusted us, the mothers to care for the baby for nine months.

For you formed my inward parts: you knitted me together in my mother's womb. I praise you, for I am fearfully and wonderfully made. Psalm 139:13-16

When I had my last couple of kids, I was considered, "high risk" due to my age and because I am Epileptic. At that time, they were doing amniocentesis at five months gestation. I told them, I didn't need one, it would not matter to me the outcome. They convinced me that it would be better to know if there were complications before the birth of the baby so that they could anticipate the needs of my baby and me. That made sense, so I had it done. Well, all was well, and I had regular deliveries. But, thinking back I wonder if I was another woman and I had found out something was wrong, would they have told me it would be best to terminate the pregnancy? We are so brainwashed into not questioning our Doctors and following their advice without question, that many babies' lives may be ended in this way. Only, later does the poor mom and dad struggle with the remorse and guilt. The idea that we, or Drs., know more than God or can anticipate the worst and then decide not to trust in God to find the silver lining, is scary and disgusting.

In my family girls seem to be the most prominent gender, only girls. Now, these couples might have tried three or four different times, hoping for the other gender, but they ultimately believe that God knows and gives us what we need. It is not always what we think we want. We need to thank God for all blessings good and bad. Even when it seems dark and begs the question, "Why me?" there will be a silver lining. This includes unexpected or unwanted pregnancies. We don't or can't always know at the time what that blessing may be, but it will be shown to us later, and we will feel it. It takes faith and love of Christ. That trust can be hard when it comes to personal losses. Having that trust also gives us hope for the future. I know it is easy to say, but we have to live it too and put our faith in Christ.

We know that all things work for good for those who love God. Roman 8: 28

All things. Really, all things? I think of Pope John Paul II after he was shot. He immediately forgave his assailant, wanted to see him in person, and eventually, he converted him. The mercy and love he showed him was indeed Gods mercy. It seems impossible, but I bet Pope John Paul slept easier at night not harboring bitterness.

Since I became a Catholic, I have changed my views on the death penalty. I used to think that it was okay. An eye for an eye and all that, they deserved it. But, who am I to say, when someone should die. Christ hung on that cross and felt ALL of our sins; past, present, and future. I will certainly, not be the one to show no mercy.

I know I am on earth to do Gods will and show Christ to other people. Is that always easy? No, but that is why we pray for help from God. God can give us the grace to accept what we find unacceptable. He will find that silver lining for us. He is God! There is nothing he cannot do. We have to accept that his time frames may be different than ours, his answer may be different than what we asked for and that a No answer, is an answer.

The Catholic church has a group called Project Rachel Ministry-HopeAfterAbortion.org. This group supports men and women that have in some way been harmed by or made the mistake of taking the life of an unborn child. I know that many men and women feel regret or remorse and don't think that they can get past or continue to feel that hole in their heart over what decisions they made. But that is not true. Our God is a merciful God. He loves and forgives us, for anything. We only have to ask for his forgiveness and open our hearts to his will for us. We are never alone.

If ever in despair remember this scripture;

For I am convinced that neither death, nor life, nor angels, nor principalities, nor present things, nor future things, nor powers, nor height, nor depth, nor any other creature will able to separate us from the love of God in Christ Jesus our Lord. Romans 8:38-39

PRAYER LIFE

Here, there and everywhere

P rayer life meant two things to me before I became Catholic; 1) Petitioning God- Asking for things or 2) Sunday service and rote prayers.

The more I exposed myself to faith, to Mass, to songs of praise and to learning from others, the more ways I found there are to pray. I love to learn how others pray; there is no one formula. No real guide book or a method that makes it more comfortable, but different ways are more appealing than others to me. I also tend to change my prayer life like I pick up new crafts to do. I love to learn new things, and then I move on to something else. I have painted, made jewelry, soap, and candles, knitted, crocheted and done macramé, sewed, collected, painted stones, grafted plants, gardened and canned, variety is excellent. I am getting smarter though. Now, before I buy a lot of support products, to make me the expert that I dream of becoming, I like to try things first. My passion currently is collecting religious paintings, medals, and rosaries at auctions. Glenn can be thankful I still want to cook, clean and travel or he would be one unhappy guy.

As far as my prayer life and habits, I have practiced many different religious meditations and change what I read in the morning frequently. I love to learn from other people's experiences and realize we are made from the same mold and are trying to develop or maintain our relationship with God. Looking for new ways to strengthen our devotions and learn and share with others will provide new ways to build our relationship with God. If you have been looking for an everyday read, choose the Magnificat. It is a little daily book that has the daily Mass in it and can be ordered. It is like a church service at home and has all of the daily readings, Psalms, meditations, feast of the day and usually a story to interest you. That monthly subscription is very inclusive, and you are participating in the same scriptures that every Catholic church is reading that day. The Magnificat is the right size to fit in your purse or lunch box? Okay, briefcase. No, I have it, diaper bag, that's it, just put it in there.

An alternative to reading and praying can be to some-times just listening. Listening for God. Yes, people do have conversations with God. That was a revelation for me. I was not brought up talking with God. I don't remember any time where I was told to turn to prayer for an answer, yet, that is what I do all the time now. It works for me in so many ways. First, I get answers I may not have thought of; second, I can relax my control and allow God to steer my decisions. I was never big on micromanaging or thinking that only I had all of the answers. I may have had a clue, but I still wanted to hear what others thought. At work getting buy-in was the key to success. It was better to elicit cooperation than impose negative consequences. No one wants to work in a system that does not allow free thinking.

My first job was as a hospital housekeeper, and some of the things I learned from that job have served me well. I might have been only the housekeeper but even the Head Nurse at the time asked for my opinion, and she accepted it as valid. One afternoon she asked me if I couldn't sweep the ICU, which was one of my daily tasks. I said, "Sure, but I did sweep this morning." That answer stopped her in her tracks, and she said, "Oh, then I will inform my nurses to not drop so much on the floor during the day, they need to be more careful." Years later when I was a nurse, I knew how those nurses could quickly drop stuff on the floor, with the opening of IV tubing, medication, bandages, it was nonstop ripping papers and tossing near the trash can, and I reminded myself to try to sink my shots, rather than bounce off the rim. My station in the job force did not define me. I have always tried to remember that when working with all groups of people. Everyone wants a piece of the pie, no matter how small their piece of pie is. When I make a chocolate cream pie or cherry pie at our family gatherings, I had better cut it into one-inch slices. If only eight pieces are cut, there are so many unhappy folks wanting their slice of the pie.

Prayer is not difficult; it is more of a habit. Like any well-developed habit, it takes repeating. Even now, seven years after I have retired I wake up at five am, I am programmed. That is how we must hone our prayer life and also include it during the day, not just in the morning. During my day, when I am thankful, I thank God. When I am worried, I ask for Gods help. When I am saying goodbye, I often say, God, love you with a hug. When I am relieved I will say, Thanks be to God! When I want to share God's mercy and love I will often say, God, Bless you. These phrases are now part of my everyday vocabulary. We have God to thank for all good or bad. There is nothing that we do or go through that God is not aware of, can't get over or bring us some good from. He is the Master of Silver Linings.

One of the most vibrant forms of prayers are the hymns. I find myself humming, "Open my eyes, Lord" many days. There are hymns I can't sing without choking up. I get emotional because I can relate to the lyrics, " Be not Afraid" is one of them. It brings me back to that life-changing day that God spoke to me through my vision of St. John Paul II. There are many other beautiful hymns, and we learn them because we attend Mass regularly. Before I did this, I never hummed hymns. I didn't know many; and it isn't appropriate to hum Silent Night all year.

The Catholic faith has many novena's, which are nine-day prayers, there are chaplets, or daily reads that we can start and stop anytime. They keep us connected during the week and help us to hopefully live the Gospel for the day. Then there are all the saints! Saints have prayers attached to them because they are known for their specific strengths. Saints often have a prayer card assigned to them with a prayer that you can read over. The other thing about Saints that we all need to remember is that they are Saints. They reside in heaven, and they pray. They pray for us. We can pray through them to Jesus. Saints are known for different things. When the saints are remembered for something particular, they can be deemed patron Saints of that issue. There is St Rita, the patron saint of abused women, who is associated with helping them. Some countries have a Patron Saints; Mexico has the Virgin of Guadalupe because she appeared to a poor Mexican in 1531. Her statue can also be found in many Catholic churches.

When anyone joins the Catholic church, they select a Saint, for their patron, one that represents something personal or unique to that particular person. This could be how they feel, or how they want to live or someone they admire. I chose Veronica when I joined the Catholic church as my patron saint. Veronica is the woman in the sixth Station of the Cross who wipes the face of Jesus. That caring, loving picture of a stranger helping another resonated with me. As a nurse, I wanted to feel that empathy and compassion to those in need even when it was a challenge. She is a perfect saint for me to this day, as I like to listen and help others. When raising a large family or just having a large family there are many times to exercise peacemaking skills. She is a good reminder that one can never give up, but do what is right. Choosing your patron Saint is an essential benchmark in the Catholic journey and not to be taken lightly. Everyone studies many saints to find their match before selecting one in particular to be their patron saint.

Then there is always the Saint of the Day or the Feast of the Day. So many ways to enrich your prayer life without much effort. Most of the little prayer books fit in my purse. I can pull one out and read it, instead of Facebook or something less meaningful than that.

Pray without ceasing. 1 Thessalonians 5:17

I am not going to say I ever accomplish this, but it is a great goal. Can you imagine if we did this, there would be no crime, only good things would happen?

When I was a Home Care Nurse, one of my clients was an elderly man that lived alone. He was a Catholic convert, and he prayed five to seven rosaries a day. He had such faith. He fell at one point and laid on the floor for four days before a daughter came to check on him. I asked him how he survived that. Wasn't he scared? He told me that he had his rosary and gave his life to the Blessed Mary and it was like he slept for the four days. He had no recollection of the pain or misery that he must have endured. He said he wouldn't be alive without his faith. Just hearing him tell me his story was a gift from God to me. What a great guy.

An easy way to learn about the Lord is through Catholic radio stations. I have Sirius radio in my car, and that is all I listen to. I learn of new books that I may be interested in, common questions that are answered, or dilemmas that I need help with. I also, learn about what the Pope is doing, the Church, the scandals, the local services. Well, just about everything Catholic. Staying immersed in the message, keeps my head clear and my thoughts in the right place. We all need help to keep on the path. I am not going to do it myself. It takes the grace of God and the words of people that he speaks through. After you listen to a couple of different programs, you will learn which one's appeal to you most and then follow those. I don't listen to anything annoying or not helpful to me. Catholic radio is not a penance. It is inspirational, and you will find you want to share what you have heard.

We must remember that any prayer that we pray is a thanksgiving. Even the simplest, "Praise God." The bottom line with prayer is, PRAY. You don't have to be in need or trouble to pray. A prayer of gratitude because you are happy is heaven bound too, speaking of heaven bound. There are always questions about why Catholics use incense or more accurately, so MUCH incense. We like to think that our burning of incense facilitates our prayers being carried to heaven on its smoke. Glenn and I like incense and we have a small incense burner on our home altar. The smell of sweet myrrh or Damascus rose to waft throughout the house is almost purifying, cleansing.

The other scent that is pleasing is the burning of the beeswax candles. We obtain them from the annual Candlemas service. Technically, Candlemas is the feast day for the Presentation of the Lord at the Jewish temple. This would be forty days after Jesus' birth. At our church, it is the time when we can obtain the beeswax candles for our homes. The candles not only smell fantastic and are dripless but are blessed. Perfect for lighting during our morning quiet times or if I ever have the nerve to invite a priest over. That sounds funny, but it is a big thing for me. Priests aren't even judgmental and would be very happy to be invited over. It probably stems back to when I was eleven, and the Episcopal priest made an unexpected house call to our home. Our family had been out in the yard, clearing and burning brush all day and we were smoky, dirty and tired. The last thing my folks expected that day was the priest to pull into the drive. I must have sensed the tension as a child because to this day, that is what I feel at the thought of a priest visiting.

Prayer, there is not a wrong or right way. The only thing wrong is if we don't pray, don't include God in our lives, our decisions or marriage. My kids will call me for advice and I give it, but I often say, "turn it over to God and pray about it," See what feels right to you." How do you know the answer you hear is from God? What I think is if the answer makes you feel easier, more comfortable and has some relation to scripture, it probably is okay. God is not going to give us advice that is against his teachings or that makes us take an action that is harmful to us in the long run. Let's say the question is, "Should I buy a new car? ". We can get carried away at the moment talking with the salesperson about miles per gallon, the color of the car or roominess. At least that is what I consider. The thing is, we must do our homework with God before we get in that emotional state of… it's the last yellow car in the world, someone else will get it, or it feels so roomy. At some point, I should have worked a payment into my budget and figured the top dollar I could pay. When we go shopping for a car, and the salesman tries to car talk with Glenn. He steers them to me and says, " You have to convince her; she knows what she will pay." Then the conversation takes a whole new turn. I love that moment. I am pretty unbendable with the resources God has given me, and it is evident very quickly to the salesperson. Final answer, "Pray first, not afterward." Resources are finite and paying bills is not a loaves and fishes experience.

Lectio Divina is an insightful way to pray. I went to a Spiritual Counselor, a religious person at Nazareth a couple of years back and first became exposed to this process. We would first set quiet and ask the Holy Spirit for guidance. Then we each would read the Sundays Gospel, slowly and almost meditatively. I am trying to see what "popped" out from the words. What was God saying to me? When I would finish, I would pray quietly about it, and different words or phrases would repeat themselves in my mind. These thoughts would be what I would bring forward to the counselor to discuss. She facilitated the conversation without really leading the dialogue. She could tie in my thoughts with other scripture many times to lend support, and she always would help me with a game plan to manage any concerns. I found this method of praying extremely useful. Currently, Glenn is in the two-year training to become a Spiritual Counselor, and hopefully, there will be a counselor at every Catholic parish.

When we allow God to speak to us or as they say to whisper in our ear, we will hear him. But, we first must seek him, open our hearts to him and rest quietly.

The moral is, we are not in control. The sooner that is realized, and we humble ourselves to our Creator the better we all will be. The other thing I think I need mention is we need to hear the word of God, and by this, I mean read the word of God. He has spoken many times in the Bible. Some Bibles have that Jesus says in red font. When pick that Bible up, it will be straightforward to see God's words. When you read what Jesus has to say, substitute whoever he is talking to for yourself. Put yourself in the parable or the narrative. In the parable of the Prodigal son, sometimes I am the father who forgives all, sometimes the eldest son who must learn to be humble, show mercy, share and forgive, and many times the returning son who expects nothing and is overwhelmed by the generosity of others. It becomes more personal and is easier to relate to what God is telling us. After all, he is talking to you and me.

If you need a more formal method to pray there is always; Adoration, Contrition, Thanksgiving, Supplication/Petition.

Start by adoring God-Thank you Lord for your many mercies towards me. Pray silently, with your eyes on Jesus.

Contrition- I am so sorry for not spending the time I should with you. You mean more to me than anything, I will do better.

Thanksgiving- Thank you, Jesus, for the health in my family, for the long life of my parents, the many grandchildren I am blessed with, all of the Priests devotions, the many churches we can attend, my income, my faith.

Petition- Lord, please give me the strength to forgive past injuries, increase my faith, show me the direction you want my faith to lead me and to always be kind and loving in your name.

Finish with- I asked this in Jesus' name, Father, Son, and Holy Spirit.

Lastly, pray for your spouse. It is said that we are responsible for praying our spouse into heaven. I am not sure where I heard that, but I like it. I know, I know, that can't be entirely true. In any relationship, it helps with forgiveness and understanding if you are praying for them. When I first started to pray, I didn't know how to pray except for me, me, me. Then I learned to pray for others first, the unborn, the dying, our leaders, daily decisions, the fallen away, teens struggling with faith, those underemployed, our priests, the sanctity of marriage, my family, the health of my parents, my special intentions and the intentions of others. You can see, by praying for others, one could be praying all day. There is so much to pray for that doesn't involve my petitions; give me strength, help me lose weight, the courage to do the right thing, better health, less temper, no gossip, be more generous, attend church more. You get it. Prayer really can be unceasing. Thanks be to God.

RECONCILIATION

When being best buds with God is not enough

That used to be me. I was "friends" with God, and I would say, "Sorry, God" and thought that we were right, boy, was I missing the boat. Later, I found out God knew what he was doing by creating the Sacrament of Reconciliation.

In Reconciliation or Confession, there is education, healing, and absolution of the sin. Without the intervention of the priest, who is standing in for God how are we to learn a new way of dealing with a sin, a bad habit? We can't pardon our sins, that has never worked. We often require a new game plan, something we hadn't thought of, some new strategies to help to avoid the same problems repeatedly. That is where the education component comes in. Priests are very learned men. Many have master's degrees before they even enter the seminary. They will also be the first to tell you, that there is nothing under the sun that they haven't heard or helped people with. You cannot shock a priest; this is a good thing.

The Priest has experience and knowledge of knowing what may work as far as changing behavior's and also how to help us learn to forgive ourselves. The absolution they provide is God's absolution, His forgiveness. His mercy allows us to leave the confessional with a clean slate and we can start our lives fresh, most likely with a new approach to living our lives.

Reconciliation is not a secular idea; it was Jesus's, and it should be something we do.

You are Peter, and upon this rock, I will build my church, and the gates of the netherworld shall not prevail against it. I will give you the keys to the kingdom of heaven. Whatever you bind on earth shall be bound in heaven: and whatever you loose on earth shall be loosed in heaven. Matthew 16:18-19

As Catholics, it is quite easy for us because we all have a pamphlet with what sins require confession. This pamphlet has questions you ask yourself to see if you have committed them. When, you answer, Yes, that would be something you need to confess. I heard someone say; I can't think of anything to confess. I smile because we always can confess that we don't put the Lord first, which is breaking the 1st commandment, to Love the Lord above all else. If I think of the number of hours I watch TV compared to the number of hours I pray, I have to acknowledge I break that commandment daily. There are also particular times in the church week that a priest hears confession, or we can make an appointment with a priest for a time that better suits us, or maybe we haven't been to confession in a long time and have a lot to confess, so will need more time. Reconciliation is always available for those who seek it and so is the grace that we obtain from this sacrament.

Whenever I begin to think I may not need confession. I remember that even the Pope goes to confession, what is it, weekly or monthly? Our priests confess monthly if not more. Now, I have to assume they lead a more upright life than me, but they are compelled to go. Are they just more honest, I doubt that they are more sinful than me, although they would be the first to call themselves sinners. It is valid for me, the more I go, the easier it is to go. I tend to remember things I wanted to say. If I don't go for three months, I may be wracking my brains for something significant to confess. But the truth is, if I go over each day when I lay down at night I can highlight several areas that could have been handled differently. Anytime you are in a relationship, go to work, drive your car, you have more than enough opportunities to do things a better way. These may be things you can bring to confession. Confession is always a must before Mass if you missed a Sunday at church. Sunday's and Holy Days of Obligations are mandatory. God gave us one day to rest and spells it out in the Bible. Remember the 10 Commandments? On that day he wants us to attend church.

We must consider how to rouse one another to love and good works.

We should not stay away from our assembly, as is the custom of some, but encourage one another, and this all the more as you see the day drawing near. Hebrews 1-: 24-25

If we are sick or unable to attend for some reason, that is permissible. But, when we willfully choose to miss church because of poor planning or laziness, then Reconciliation is required.

Glenn and I like to go on cruises, and you will find that many Sundays are sea days with no church on site. On an Alaskan cruise at one port, the Catholic church had a van at the dock to take parishioners to Mass. We took advantage of that rather than an excursion into town, because it was such a privilege. That was fantastic, but it was unusual while on a cruise ship, and that church had the foresight and motivation to help fellow Catholics attend there Mass. When we were in Lisbon, Portugal on a cruise we took the Fatima excursion because we knew we could go to Mass and secondly because of the shrine itself. That was the best excursion of the cruise, and there were many to choose from. You see, it is a choice and free will. Choose wisely when you have the opportunities.

There are many things to love about Reconciliation. The first of course is absolution from God. The second to me is the wealth of knowledge or varied responses that come from the different priest. Some priests are very biblical. They quote a bible passage that is relevant and then link your penance to saying or reading something from the Bible. Another priest will commiserate but offer advice or a piece of knowledge that helps to understand the sin. All of the priests I have confessed to have been very concerned, empathetic and kind. They will help you through the reconciliation process if you have forgotten what to do or ask you questions if you want them to jog your memory of a forgotten sin. After the confessing is done, your act of contrition and the final absolution by the priest, he will give you a penance to complete once you leave the confessional. When you leave the confessional, your sins are forgiven. You feel great, much cleaner than when you went in. All burdens should be off your shoulders. The priest has taken them on, for God. Your job is to let go of the burdens. Trust that Jesus can handle them for you. You no longer own them. That is sometimes the hardest thing to do; we are so controlling. Letting God take over is that simple if we let go.

For those that don't go to confession, but talk to God, I don't think there is that feeling of relief, and there has been no absolution. The process of humbling yourself into sharing your dirty laundry with another person is beneficial to you. We all have a hard time letting our pride go. Pride is not a virtue. It is the opposite of a virtue. The virtue is humility. It is good to cultivate virtues; it brings us closer to God.

14

PURGATORY

Who needs that?

W hen I was a young child, my mom would always announce dinner was almost ready by saying, "Wash up, dinner is about to be served and come to the table." It was clear to us kids that mom did not think we were clean enough to sit at the table. These were the times when we all ate together, using knives, spoons, and forks and had napkins. Everyone sat together, ate together and no one left the table unless they asked to be "Excused." You prepared for dinner. That is similar to purgatory. Dinner is heaven and purgatory is washing up.

Purgatory is a Catholic thing. It is a process not a place. This process is a cleansing of sins before going to heaven. When you think about how we are at our time of death, we are nowhere near perfect enough to be in the presence of God. We must be cleansed, totally, of anything unworthy of God. The examples of how one should act, look, or not look or even dress in the presence of God are throughout the Bible.

> God said, "Come no nearer!" Remove the sandals from your feet, for the place where you stand is holy ground. Genesis 3: 5

> Uzzah reached out his hand to the ark of God and steadied it, for the oxen were making it tip. But the Lord was angry with Uzzah; God struck him on that spot, and he died there before God. 2 Samuel 6:6-8

It is said, one cannot look on God in their unclean state, or they will be struck dead. Purgatory is the place of purification so that we can be in proximity to God in heaven.

We sometimes may joke that doing good deeds on earth may shorten our time in Purgatory, but we all believe we must complete the process of cleansing before heaven.

We also pray for our dead. We pray that the dead will move on from purgatory to heaven.

> But if someone's work is burned up, that one will suffer loss: the person will be saved, but only as through fire. 1 Corinthians 4:15

15

ART, STATUES, AND ICONS, OH MY

So many ways to see and love God

Over the last ten years, we have collected many old prints, religious statues and I recently painted an icon of St Michael. We have these treasures on the walls, in the yard, aligning shelves or sitting on the floor of our house. This may seem strange to non-Catholics, but everyone seems to get used to it after a while. I used to be embarrassed by the Blessed Mother at the walk of our house and thought no one would want to walk by her that wasn't Catholic. But, my little Joysa demonstrated the love that children have for Her by often walking over the landscape to her and hugging her. In May, Joysa would remove the May flower crown the Blessed Mary was wearing and don it herself and then put it back on Our Lady's head.

If it wasn't the Blessed Mother greeting you it might have been St. Francis on the other end of the entry, holding his birds. Then there was the yard Rosary strung between the two but not touching either of them. It has taken a while, but everyone seems oblivious to them now. In fact, they have been there long enough to be painted a couple of times.

When visiting Catholic churches on our vacations or just around town, there are many differences and experiences of the senses. One of the features of our Catholic faith is the beautiful stain glass windows that depict the parables, saints, and sacraments. At St. Joseph there are long windows with colored glass panels in them on the side of the altar, and when the sun is shining, the colors stream across the altar area. This serene, rainbow of colors and the warmth of the church are a few of my first memories of St. Joe. I loved that the church was bright and colorful, not dark and cavernous. At St. Jerome in Battle Creek the stained glass is prettiest in the winter during a snowfall. The snow coming down is visible through the stained glass. This scene plays out behind the altar. The beauty of stained glass is why Glenn created the faux stained glass for our house.

Another thing of beauty is the variety of art works depicting the fourteen Stations of the Cross around the walls in different churches. Stations of the Cross can be of simple wood design; others are three-dimensional figures; others are paintings; some are more symbolic. Then there are the Baptismal fonts. Many have heated Holy water, some are walk-in for full immersion, many are large bowls of Holy Water with a fountain circulating the water. I am always curious if it will be in front of the church or the back as we enter.

He said to them, "Go into the whole world and proclaim the gospel to every creature, whoever believes and is baptized will be saved: whoever does not believe will be condemned. Mark 16: 15

Then, of course, there are the small Holy water containers at each entry to bless yourself before entering the church and leaving. You make the sign of the cross from your forehead to your heart and then across your shoulders from left to right. Making the sign of the cross, we say, "In the name of the Father and of the Son and the Holy Spirit. Amen". It prepares us to receive the grace of God and participate in what God has in store for you.

As far as statues many Catholic families have an Our Lady statue in their yard or a St. Andrew, as we do. I think it might be a deterrent to visitors from the Jehovah Witness; they seem to drive by our house. At church there is the Blessed Mary statue to the left of the altar and St. Joseph is to the right of the altar. In the areas of these statues, there are kneelers to pray or votive candles to light for a loved one. Lighting these candles with a grandchild is a teaching moment and very special. It teaches them to pray for others, and they feel so unique and important with this duty. Then when they sit back in their seats, the lit candle reminds them and all of the church that we are praying for someone.

We have a large Spanish population at our church, and on the Spanish feast days, the Blessed Mary statue will be decked out in flowers or ribbons, very colorful, beautiful. The Blessed Mary is very dear to Mexicans as it the Lady of Guadalupe is Mexico's patron saint.

On the feast of St. Joseph everyone brings food for the church pantry and His area will be filled with sacks of food. Then during the school week, the schoolchildren will each pick up a bag and take it to the food pantry. That is quite a relief; there are thousands of pounds of food. In the spring the congregation all bring a geranium to be planted, and the altar area will be red with flowers. Our parish has 1400 families, and they are very generous. There is a group of seventy-year-old women that do all the planting. I swear they have the endurance of angels and don't whine or complain. Jobs just get done.

There is pageantry in the Catholic church. The men have a group called the Knights of Columbus that do service works. They were initially formed to protect the Pope and so they have swords and quite an outfit, with tuxedos and hats with white ostrich plumes. The men are called Knights, and their wives are called Ladies of the Knights. I know, I had to get used to that title. I am a Lady of the Knight because Glenn is a fourth-degree Knight. My maternal grandfather, grandpa Hagan, was a Knight and Glenn is honored to have his sword. When the Bishop comes to our church for a special occasion or a Knight has a funeral, the Knights of Columbus gather and march into escort the priests. It is regal and elegant and should not be missed if you can be there.

This may be a good segue into the whole Sit, Stand and Kneel rationale. It is quite simple. We sit to listen, stand to acclaim and kneel to pray. During the Mass, we will be seated for the readings and homily and psalms. During the Nicene Creed, the Gospel and Lord's Prayer we stand, and we kneel during the liturgy of the Mass or breaking of the bread. The Gospel is read by the Deacon or Priest, and during this reading, we make the sign of a cross using our thumbs on our forehead, lips and over our hearts. This gesture is imprinting the Word of God on our minds, lips, and hearts. During the Mass the priest represents Christ and when the acolytes approach the altar, they bow to him, out of respect. If you ever need a cue on what you should be doing, just look at what the priest is doing, it is a good idea to follow his lead.

GIFTS OF THE HOLY SPIRIT

Why we are good at some things more than others.

The Holy Spirit is the part of the Trinity that God left with us after Jesus was resurrected. God knew we would need an Advocate, a comforter and teacher, a counselor. God knew our weaknesses and that we would need a comforter.

> And I will ask the Father, and he will give you another helper; to be with you forever. John 14:16

Living in this world and abiding the commandments to this day is complex, challenging and impossible without the grace of God. It is much easier to take the path that does not follow the commandments.

> "Enter through the narrow gate; for the gate is wide and the road broad that leads to destruction, and those who enter through it are many. How narrow the gate and

constricted the road that leads to life. And those who find it are few." Matthew 7:13-14

Just looking at the last Commandment for " do not covet." Don't "envy" your neighbors' goods that sounds easy enough. We all have our taste and material things, but the attitude of "keeping up with the Jones" is so ingrained. Did it start with television? Doubtful, but advertising does make us feel like we are entitled to everything. This entitlement is broad and includes; more than we can afford, more than we deserve, more than we want or need. Even with my kids, they sometimes set unreal expectations for themselves. They often don't buy starter homes but homes that are equal to my home after thirty years of marriage. Overbuying can lead to years of making ends meet, paycheck to paycheck. My first house was a small 1 ½ story on a crowded inner-city street. We renovated the walk-in attic with its sloped ceilings into the "master" bedroom, and all of the kids shared the main floor two bedrooms. It was tight but cozy. It seemed always to need picking up, and there was nowhere to put any clutter once you picked it up. We certainly didn't have family gatherings at our house. Our immediate family filled it up, plus we shared a drive, and our neighbor was strict about cars not parking in the driveway. We had great memories there. In town there are sidewalks where the kids learned to ride their bikes, we knew our neighbors. We lived so close my old neighbor Amos would yell over to me, "Pick that baby up, she is crying." No one let their babies cry; we didn't have sleep programs to follow to get the babies to sleep all night or stay in their beds. Raising kids seemed different. Now, when I am asked, "What would you do?", my answer may seem irrelevant. I don't think today's kids can be raised the same way.

Now, as one of my daughters tells me, "Kids don't do that mom." When I was probably talking about walking home from school or turning off the TV, or telling them to play outside, or "shocker," going to church every week. Now is not the era for me to raise children, I haven't stayed current with the trends.

Nowadays, young couples buy pretty new cars; I had older cars. I had one with such a bad battery that I had to have AAA jump it two times a week. I couldn't, afford a battery! The insurance company finally sent me a letter, saying they would not cover the jump anymore, so much for roadside assistance. Their tough love made me buy a battery; It would have been cheaper for them to buy me a battery first.

Today we all have phones and are apparently on Facebook. I gave up Facebook for Lent this year, but the downside was I was missing the posting of my grandkid's pictures for forty days. The upside was, I loved not reading Facebook daily, saved time and less drama. I wonder if I missed an event invite. Oh well, no one missed me and I didn't miss Facebook.

I remember the day my daughter taught me how to text! She said, "No one calls anyone anymore, so I had to text." This is all partly true, but also partly sad. That same daughter, Lauren, now has a little boy and we have learned to do something new called Video Messaging. It is like live TV and phone combination. Every day, we see and talk to our new grandson and it is as close as we get to seeing them without "seeing" them regularly. Love it, this technology has its benefits.

We will have family get-togethers, and the kids won't be playing outside but sitting on the floor, playing phone games against each other or showing each other the latest app. That has replaced conversation. Well, not entirely. Now, the kids seem like they are small adults and sit with the adults and participate in adult conversations. There is no longer a "kids table" at dinner anymore. I have to remind the kids to leave the big chairs for the adults. By big chairs, I mean the couch. Grandpa won't say anything but at eighty-nine does he have to sit on a hard chair. My grandkids are all great kids, courteous and kind but they are like little adults. Maybe that is how children survive these days. I don't think they are unusual in this; times are different.

Speaking of all life's many dilemmas, do you wonder we need a Holy Spirit? God is timeless; he has no past, present or future; it is all now. He knew we would have a day to day issues that we would need His grace and an advocate with Him to pull us through them. Enter the Holy Spirit. Some say, Holy Ghost. I have used both.

I understand the Holy Spirit a lot better now that I am Catholic and expect more of our relationship. Well, when God left us the Holy Spirit he intended for us to have help. Our lives are of no surprise to God. He will always know what we need, now or in our future. I have shared one of the Gifts of the Spirit as the Tears of the Holy Spirit. I think the tears of the Holy Spirit, at least for me was to demonstrate there something besides myself "out" there. Someone that connected on an emotional level with me and felt what I needed and allowed me to be who I needed to be. My experiencing that uncontrolled emotion was so "out of body" and so cleansing. I would wish everyone could go through that.

There are many gifts of the Holy Spirit. When Glenn and I attended a charismatic workshop for a couple of weeks, they spoke of the Service gifts of, expression of wisdom; expression of knowledge, faith, healing, mighty deeds, prophecy, discernment, varieties of tongues, interpretation of tongues. These were given to individuals as the Holy Spirit wished. The whole experience was, well, I am going to say it, kind of creepy. I had never experienced anyone talking in tongues or interpreting what they were saying. The prophetic gift, I could agree with. I think I have known people that can tell you of something that may happen, and it comes true. The healing gifts of people can be seen in medicine and nursing. The laying on of hands, Therapeutic Touch, much of holistic medicine can be a gift of the Holy Spirit. Mighty deeds we hear about on the news during emergencies, when people acquire superhuman strength and adrenalin takes over. The acts that heroes are remembered for. Just the gift of a mighty deed that turns you into a hero must be the grace of God working through the Holy Spirit. If people took the time to analyze or think through what courageous act they were about to do, I doubt there would be as many heroes and acts of heroism. We would talk ourselves right out of it, by weighing the odds of success.

Speaking in tongues is very intriguing. When I first heard this, it came from charismatic Catholic groups, not Pentecostal. At least that is what I heard happens a lot at a Pentecostal church. I haven't been. Now, when I hear someone say the word charismatic, I think of the gifts of the Holy Spirit, specifically, speaking in tongues. Many Popes or priests are charismatic. When the person is speaking in tongues, they have had interpreters there to authenticate the dialect, and it is interpreted as the language spoken at Christ time. Wouldn't that be Aramaic? Scholars have recorded these people and then understood what they said and compared it to what the person that had the gift of interpretation was saying and it would be the same. That in itself is miraculous. Glenn and I were not blessed with that gift. It was said, that you could be resistant if you didn't allow yourself to embrace it. I don't think I tried to be stubborn but neither did I try to make it happen. I felt if I was to have that gift, it should come without prompting by me. So, to date, I don't speak in tongues.

The fruits of the Holy Spirit are like the actions of your gifts of the Holy Spirit. These actions are very relatable they are; love, joy, peace, patience, kindness, goodness, and faithfulness. When we feel these fruits, they are coming from the Holy Spirit. Each of us may have a more substantial supply of one or the other of these gifts. If we think about our personalities or what makes us most comfortable we can most likely say which fruit of the Spirit we are rich in.

I recently took a Spiritual Gifts Inventory to see where my faith may lead me or how I could make the best use of my spiritual gifts once I knew what they were. My top seven gifts were an encouragement, evangelism, faith, giving, hospitality, intercessory prayer, mercy, and writing. I was not surprised at this outcome, but so happy it did not involve teaching or knowledge. You would think I would like to teach, being a nurse by training, but, nope. I don't want to be in front of people like that. The knowledge gift or book learning was never my strong suit. I read by skimming down the center of the page; it is not comprehensive by any means. I like my education fed to me like a child by listening or attending something and listening, or I learn by doing.

Upon examining the spiritual gifts that were in my wheelhouse, I can see them. As a nurse, I did encourage others and have mercy towards them in their healing. I don't know how evangelistic I am, but I have been involved with sharing my faith since I became a Facebook member. Once for a whole year, I did a daily mediation, which I started in Lent and which incorporated the Bible and the Catechism to a Facebook group and tried to make it interactive. I am not sure I succeeded with that; it was usually me doing all of the sharing. But, there were about forty followers, and I learned a lot that year because I was committed to finishing. I learned I could stick with something for a year. That was outstanding! Truthfully, I hadn't compared the Catechism of the Catholic Church to the Bible before that, and it opened my eyes as to many of the whys, when's and what's of the Church. The next year I felt confident enough to share spiritual books, interesting daily reads, and generally anything I found insightful and educating. I would start by praying for guidance and also that maybe one person would gain something that could bring them closer to Jesus thru the faith insights that we shared.

My Holy Spirit fruit of Hospitality is not a surprise. We have a lot of family parties, and it is either me or my brother, Anson that share in this never-ending invitation to dinner. When we were growing up, mom and dad would host the annual Hibbard-Hagan "pig roast" on their farm in Joppa. I put pig roast, in a quotation, because the entre moved from pig to beef to chicken to potluck over the years. Both sides of the family, all the neighbors, and our friends would attend, and I was usually in charge of putting together the kid's games. Which were never just for kids, everyone wanted to see their dad do the egg toss. The fruit of hospitality must run in my family.

Do not neglect hospitality, for through it some have unknowingly entertained angels. Hebrews 13: 1-2

Once, I was complaining to a coworker that we had a party, birthday or something every other week and never seemed to have a day free. She looked me in the eye and said, "Chris, that is a blessing. I have no one and no parties." From that day on, I have had a different opinion of parties. Yes, they are work, they may be expensive. But they are often the glue that holds generations together. When cousins grow up and have their kids, everyone starts their party circles, and then we lose touch. I guess that is inevitable, but I remedied that some with my entry into the Facebook world. Yes, now I still communicate with cousins in Utah or old friends from childhood. Facebook can get credited with enhancing my hospitality needs. Before that technology, I had lost years of communication with geographically distant family members.

As for the giving fruit of the Holy Spirit, I am a firm believer in the adage of "not taking it with you." I am always telling my parents, "spend it." I wish they would be a new car or even get an iPhone. Where my parents saved, I think I spend. I don't see it as spending as much as if I have the money I give it. Why not? So much giving can be done on-line routinely so I never even notice it is gone. When I used to use weekly envelopes for the church collection, it seemed I was always running out of money to put in it by Friday. Then I would be failing to give to the Lord, what I had planned. If that happens to you, go online. Glenn doesn't ask me what I give; he is happy that he doesn't have to go online, I am sure. It was odd at first to not put our envelope in the collection plate, week after week. I don't want people thinking we give nothing. But then, it is between God and us.

Giving is not just monetary. Time and talent are just as crucial as treasure. When someone seems down and talks to me about not knowing what to do, I often will tell them to, volunteer. Of course, if they need professional help, I may say that too, no worries. Volunteering brings you great joy, and you realize how good you have it. It can be quite habit-forming. The endorphins must kick in when you feel nurtured by others. Then there are the people called to be priests and religious, and others called to lead organizations that could benefit from their assistance. These are gifts and putting the fruits of those gifts into loving others.

I am living and using the gifts that the Holy Spirit gave me. My life is a blessing.

GUARDIAN ANGELS

Your name is what?

W e had an OUIGI board at our house when growing up. At that time, I didn't think of it as a bad thing. My friends and I would, of course, ask it about all the essential elements that eleven and twelve-year olds are interested in if we would have a boyfriend or who liked us? Life changing knowledge in the hands of puberty, the heavy stuff. We didn't know there was a world peace issue going on. Since becoming Catholic, I no longer read Astrology, pay any regard to my being a Gemini or play on the OUIGI board. When I take time to ponder the why's of not opening doors to the dark side, it all makes sense. I didn't have a strong sense of heaven and hell, so I never considered that the devil would relish an opportunity to enter my perfect world, through a game.

Today, I try to avoid negative experiences in general. I don't have to seek opportunities to see the dark side; life itself is full of dark paths we can wander. I have seen enough movies or read accounts of exorcism's and know that devils, ghosts, demons and now guardian angels are real. If you believe in the devil, it only makes sense that you must believe in God. No matter what you may call your God, your higher power. The insight that there is something besides us on earth and that we are a creation of such a being. One thing we can all agree on is that life is ever-changing, and that change is always caused by something; nothing can change on its own. The only unchanging thing is God.

If you believe in God, then it's not a far stretch to believe in Gods dominion of angels. Even the devil and his demons are fallen, angels. I never thought much about a Guardian Angel, especially not one assigned to me. It seemed a myth or fairy tale. Something one tells children to keep them in line.

I am known to be a stumbler. I fall probably once a month, just tripping over my own feet. I have fallen downstairs, barely hurting myself, off bleachers, just embarrassed and once one other time I fell in the woods and cracked my elbow. Not a bad break, just enough to keep me from typing very fast at work. When we visited the Grand Canyon, Glenn was so afraid I would fall in, by accident.

Last fall I was walking through the woods on one of our paths. On the trails, there are often old roots or stumps, and so I try to watch out for them. Typical of me, I hit one and stumbled forward and yelled, "Help me, Phillip!" I was able to catch myself and recover before I fell to the ground, and so I didn't fall that time. Or did I catch myself, did I have help? I stopped walking, stood there and said to myself, "What did I just say?" I thought about it and repeated; I said, " Help me, Phillip!" I don't know any Phillips. My husband is Glenn, but he wasn't with me. Then it struck me that I must have a guardian angel named, Phillip. I tried to shake off the name, thinking. Phillip wasn't a very cool, guardian angel name. Maybe, Gabriel or Michael, but, no, I knew in my heart that my guardian angels name was Phillip.

Guardian Angels are creatures that God makes. They are a spirit and have no physical body. I am not sure how my angel, kept me from falling that day, but that's another mystery. From what I know, these angels agree to be our guardian angels and are with us from before birth until death. They are with us through every decision, good or bad, they know all of our sins, that is a scary thought. But, they do not leave us. They are dedicated to us and pray for us.

The children's night time prayer is probably the most common prayer to a guardian angel and is comforting in its safety net around us.

Angel of God, my guardian dear, to whom God's love commits me here.

Ever this night, be at my side, to light and guard, to rule and guide. Amen

We can never forget that Angel Gabriel appeared to the Blessed Virgin Mary and announced that she would conceive a son by the power of the Holy Spirit and he was to be called Jesus.

In the sixth month, the angel Gabriel was sent from God to a town of Galilee called Nazareth, to a virgin betrothed to a man named Joseph, of the house of David, and the virgin's name was Mary, And coming to her, he said, "Hail, favored one, The Lord is with you." Luke 1: 26-27

I guess I hadn't thought of him being similar to my guardian angel. We have all heard of Michael; he is an Archangel; a chief messenger and he answers to God. He cannot be summoned by us. He protects mankind from the devil.

DAILY LIFE

Keeping God in your circle of trust.

L ife has gotten more relaxed now that the kids are grown, we are retired, and our main concerns are feeding the dogs. The pace is slower, yet we always seem busy. When I was first retired, I had the go-go mentality and wanted to do everything in one day, like it was Saturday. Now, every day is Saturday; I have to be reminded what day of the week it is. Glenn, who had been retired for the year before me, had it figured out. He said, "Honey, we are retired, we don't have to do everything in one day; there is always tomorrow." That has kind of become our rule. We will make one appointment in a day, and that will "do us in." I order to save my strength and time, I now have caught on to home delivery of groceries right into the kitchen. I like to take a nap while I am "shopping," then when I get up, the delivery is here and brought into my kitchen. Our dog food is even delivered, and in the last year, I have learned how to use Amazon Prime. Not going to town, waiting in lines, fighting traffic and impulse shopping is a thing of the past for us now. That in itself is a gift from God. I feel bad that stores are closing but, then I think jobs may be shifting. It is a changing world.

What these changes have brought us is more free time at home. More time to add God to our lives. Time to write a book on faith, attend different parishes or services. Go out of town to visit the grandkids or go to their games. Our time is more our own now.

On the quiet afternoons, it is lovely to sit in our prayer room, incense in the air, listening to the daily office of reading. You would be surprised in the way God can speak to you when you are not distracted, and he is not drowned out by daily activities. I can see why people want to go for quiet walks in the woods, our fishing. Everyone needs the peace and tranquility afforded you when you have more time on your hands. We no longer have a bathroom with a tub that I could lock myself away in. Now we have a walk-in shower, that is wheelchair accessible, for whatever the future holds.

I enjoy reading inspirational books and want to share them with someone as soon as I am finished. I used to save them for my kids, but they seem to be left in the pile of "to do, when I have time," and will be left unopened in their busy lives. Maybe, they will read a book their mom writes. I can only hope. I have recently, just started leaving good reads at the chapel, like minds and all that. I figure someone that makes the time to come there will have the time to enjoy an insightful spiritual read.

I don't want you to think I have given up on our kids though. I just gave my oldest daughter, Angelin, a gift box for my grandkids for Easter and said to her," It is religious."

Kind of as a disclaimer, kids seem to be disappointed in my idea of a gift and I didn't want the kids to be disappointed. I was never so happy as when she replied, "Of course, its Easter! They know it will be religious; it is from you and grandpa". It is not a bad thing to be known as the grandparents that give religious stuff — planting the seeds.

One practice that Glenn and I started doing this year is the habit of praying together when we go to bed. After we settle in, get talked out, then, Glenn will pray. He will start with the Our Father, then Hail Mary and close with St. Michael prayer and if we have any intentional prayers we say them. This simple act of closing our day with prayers we say together is not just loving, but special and keeps us safe. We have noticed a funny/odd thing lately. Our Aussie, Teddy, is usually wedged between us when we go to bed. He will stay in that position until the prayers are over then he gets up and gets down off the bed, and sleeps on the rug, where he is a position to survey everything in the room and entering the room. Dogs are certainly not misnamed as "man's best friend"; they must have a direct link to God somewhere.

When we first started praying, we tried different prayers, but we settled on the three we choose. When I think of it, they all kind of have a different purpose and benefit us in their way. The, Our Father helps us to forgive. Is there something or someone that we need to make amends to, show a little more kindness or mercy towards and generally thank God for life. The Hail Mary prepares us for anything that can come, even our deaths, "pray for us sinners, now and at the hour of hour death." The St. Michael's prayer protects us from the devil, "Be our protection, against the wickedness

and snares of the Devil.. thrust into Hell Satan, and all the
evil spirits, who prowl about the world seeking the ruin of
souls." That word, "prowl" sends shivers through me. When
I think about the Devil, prowling about to see who is recep-
tive to him, who is weak in their faith, or the vulnerable. I
gladly, send the Archangel Michael after them while I sleep.
The last benefit of not going to sleep before prayer is we
don't go to bed angry or not talking because you can't pray
the Our Father and stay mad at anyone. What a gift God
gave us with The Lord's Prayer.

> *Our Father in heaven,*
> *Hallowed be your name,*
> *Your Kingdom come,*
> *Your will be done,*
> *On earth as in heaven.*
> *Give us today our daily bread*
> *And forgive us our debts,*
> *As we forgive our debtors,*
> *And do not subject us to the final test,*
> *But deliver us from the evil one. Amen*
> *Matthew 6:9-13*

Throughout the last ten years, I have learned more about
being a Catholic by just living my faith. I still surprise
myself when I have the answer to a question someone may
ask me about Catholicism. I never knew people had a
passion against the Catholic faith until I became one.
Catholics don't seem to be staunch defenders of their faith.
We seldom quote scripture all though we read or hear scripture every day. Our sacraments are misunderstood, yet they

seem like common sense to us. Our statues are thought to be idols by those outside of our faith and are sometimes shunned. I recently read that when Henry the VIII started the Anglican church, he chose to have statues no longer, but only two-dimensional works of art, like paintings. This may have been the beginning of the confusion with how we honor statues. Another area of confusion seems to be Our Lady the Blessed Mary. It only makes sense to me that God would choose a perfect vessel for Jesus. God is not going to dwell in anything less than perfection. This list seems endless to a new Catholic, and it is of no wonder that we fail at defending our love for the faith. I can tell you that I know in my heart, without a doubt that it is right. I may never be able to articulate sufficiently to another person, but I have no questions.

I have since learned that I don't have to have all the answers. I can find the answers, I can ask the priest, I can get back to people, but generally, people are curious and aren't listening for your replies. I feel they want me to hear them and maybe realize the error to my beliefs. I can say with confidence that I was called by the Holy Spirit. It was not a frivolous choice. I feel at home, at peace and more in love with Jesus than ever. My job is to share his love. I may not change other people's minds; only the Holy Spirit will do that. But, maybe I can take some fear away, confusion or some misinterpretation. Being a Catholic is a good thing, or Jesus would not have started this Church.

My daughter-in-law, Alyssa, who has told me, she will, "never be Catholic", has the most Catholic heart of most of my children. She would pose the most almost, adversarial questions in regard to our Catholic beliefs and I would stutter through the rational and Glenn would calmly, tell her the true answer. Boy was she a challenge to me, when I was a young Catholic. Finally, we found common ground in our love of Jesus. Our love may have come from different backgrounds, but we agreed that Jesus was Lord. I feel she saved my son through her love and her faith in God. He had a troubled youth and then he went through the Challenge program for his high school diploma. This program is an almost military boot camp style of training for six months and I was so worried about him and missed him. I would write him daily and send him prayer cards and little tips on how to pray and he graduated and was a changed man. He fell in love with Alyssa who had no time for him but he persevered until she recognized that she loved him too. Now, they thrive together sharing bible scripture, befriending the homeless and are the most charitable couple. They have also taught their daughters to know and love the Lord. They really see people and know what to do or say to them. I love that Alyssa allows me, to be me and still thinks very highly of me. We laugh about our differences, and we pray together, out loud. She makes me pray and asks for my prayers. Pulls me out of my shyness into praying aloud. People that know me will never think I am shy, but many "so called" extroverts are shy down deep. We often talk because silence is uncomfortable. I believe, she is a gift from God to my family. She has made me a better Catholic. The challenges she has given me have made us better in-laws, friends and we respect each other. Thanks be to God for Alyssa.

OUR ROAD TO EMMAUS

Were not our hearts burning within us.

On my prayer room East wall, I have a $3.00, three-foot-wide print of Jesus walking with two disciples on the road to Emmaus. The disciples did not recognize Jesus, as Jesus the Nazarene that was just crucified. They were trying to tell Jesus of the crucifixion and were astounded that he wasn't aware of it, Jesus' death was all the talk; everyone was in grief and confused by his death. This stranger had not heard anything about it. As they walked, Jesus changed their hopelessness and sorrow into more of a concern that he stay with them for the night. It had grown late, and it was time for a meal. During the meal, the disciples recognized Jesus, like Jesus during the breaking of the bread. Then there was a celebration.

And it happened that, while he was with them at table, he took bread, said the blessing, broke, and gave it to them. With that, their eyes were opened, and they recognized him, but he vanished from their sight. Then they said to each other. "Were not our hearts burning within us while he spoke to us on the way and opened the scripture to us?" Luke 24: 30-32

Isn't that how Jesus appears to us. In a stranger, as a stranger, unrecognizable as we know Him. None of us are waiting for the Jesus we see in pictures to walk up and speak to us. I think in my mind, I see him a certain way, and yes, it is probably like he looks in the embroidered Jesus picture that hangs on my den wall.

But, in reality, he has been trying to teach us that He is everyone we meet. Everyone we hear. Everyone we see. In everyone, even those we don't like. We don't want to believe that the evil of the world could be a child of God. But, it is said that God thinks of all of us as His children and will not give up on us.

"What man among you having a hundred sheep and losing one of them would not leave the ninety-nine in the desert and go after the lost one until he finds it? "And when he does find it, he set it on his shoulders with great joy and, upon his arrival home, he calls together his friends and neighbors and says to them, "Rejoice with me because I have found my lost sheep. I tell you, in just the same way there will be more joy in heaven over one sinner who repents than over ninety-nine righteous people who do not need repentance." Luke 15:4-7

I know we are not as merciful as God in His mercy, but we have God, and through his grace, we can be merciful. We don't have to be the judge and jury of evil people or of the ones that have, "done us wrong." That is God's job. That job will not go undone either. So, no worries that only we can meet out justice. Thinking that was only demonstrates our insufficient trust in God.

On our road to Emmaus, we will have many joys and heartaches. Each one will be improved by sharing the experience or the emotions with our Lord. We also benefit from walking the journey with another disciple in our lives. Someone to trust and share our love of the Lord with. Having this friend has made my faith stronger and more fruitful. I have learned more ways to love the Lord, new prayers to pray and religious books that are helpful. Many times, I just need help with explanations. The "why do we do that" kind of answers that one learns along the way. When I know why we do something, it makes the occasion more real, deeper and more understood. I firmly believe having a spiritual mentor or director helps in the growth of our faith and ultimately our relationship with God.

Along with the friend or friends in Christ that have helped to guide me on my journey, I have my companion in Christ, my Glenn. He doesn't realize how much he knows and what common sense suggestions he makes to me that smooth my path on a day to day basis. As husband and wife, we both have our roles. I cook, do laundry and clean. He changes the fuses or any other creepy thing in our old Michigan basement; he runs the generator when the power is out and keeps the driveway clear in the winter. We both like outdoor activities, so we kind of share those duties. But when we talk faith, we are equal in Gods sight and each other. He listens to me and me him. He has his liturgy of the hours, and I have my writing and intercessory prayers. We both have our ministries at church, almost always together. He enjoys being a Eucharistic Minister, and I drag my feet. I am still afraid I will drop the precious bread or have to itch my face or stumble down the step or, well you name it. It runs through my mind that it could happen to me up there on the altar. Nothing terrible has ever happened, and every time I complete it and return to my seat, I thank God, heartily. After I perform the duties of the Eucharistic Minister, I feel more love and trust because I touched the body or blood of Christ.

On our road to Emmaus, we always say grace before meals. We hold hands and Glenn prays out loud. It doesn't matter if we are in a restaurant with each other or a group. We will say grace. Same at family gatherings, it is so awkward to not start a great meal and companionship with a prayer of Thanksgiving. When I look around at the grown kids when their dad is praying, there are often sniffles. Prayer is such a gathering thing, a bringing together of people, a common thread running thru everyone at the same time, tying us to the Almighty. It is truly inspirational. Thanks be to God.

As you travel your road to Emmaus, the trials and the smiles remember you are walking step by step with Jesus. Your friendship is based on trust and commitment to an unseen but felt presence. A presence so mighty that you will hear Him when you don't want to and don't expect to but need to. You will hear Him when your mind has forgotten how He sounds when you haven't said His name out loud in prayer in years and when you think He has forgotten you. You will be reminded of Him by the people you meet, the scenery you see and the music you hear. You will know Him in the sweetness of nostalgia, it is a gift from God. The remembrance of time worth remembering, a touch, a smell, a thought, or a word.

There is nothing bigger or better in your life than God, and you will come to terms with your Lord on the road to Emmaus, and your heart will be burning with desire. May God Bless You.

ABOUT THE AUTHOR

Christine Belland is a retired Registered Nurse. She lives in rural Southwest Michigan with her husband, Glenn, and dogs, Louie and Teddy. Sit-Stand and Kneel is her spiritual journey into the Catholic faith and her first religious book. She has published a couple family recipe books and an auto-biography of her father prior to this. Spare time is devoted to her faith, family of seven grown children with grandchildren and trying new hobbies or traveling.

Made in the
USA
Columbia, SC